# MONETARY AND FINANCIAL PLANNING FOR A TRANSITORY ECONOMY

To My Uncle
Santipriya Basu

# Monetary and Financial Planning for a Transitory Economy

An adaptive control model for India

DIPAK R. BASU, M.A., Ph.D.

# Avebury
Aldershot • Brookfield USA • Hong Kong • Singapore • Sydney

© Dipak R. Basu 1995

All rights reserved. No part of this publication may be reproduced, stored in a retrieval system, or transmitted in any form or by any means, electronic, mechanical, photocopying, recording or otherwise without the prior permission of the publisher.

Published by
Avebury
Ashgate Publishing Limited
Gower House
Croft Road
Aldershot
Hants GU11 3HR
England

Ashgate Publishing Company
Old Post Road
Brookfield
Vermont 05036
USA

**British Library Cataloguing in Publication Data**

Basu, Dipak R.
 Monetary and Financial Planning for a
 Transitory Economy: Adaptive Control
 Model for India
 I. Title
 330.954

ISBN 1 85972 021 8

**Library of Congress Catalog Card Number: 95-76419**

Printed in Great Britain by Ipswich Book Co. Ltd., Ipswich, Suffolk.

# Contents

|   |   |   |
|---|---|---|
| | List of Figures | vii |
| | List of Tables | viii |
| | Preface | x |
| 1 | **India's Economic Scene and the Behaviour of the Monetary-Financial Instruments** | 1 |
| | Introduction | 1 |
| | Banking Policies and Credit Controls | 16 |
| | Industrial Policy and Licencing Systems | 18 |
| | Monetary and Financial Policies | 22 |
| | Foreign Trade, Exchange Rate and Debt | 36 |
| | New Economic Policies | 48 |
| | IMF Conditionalities and their Effects | 50 |
| | Appropriate Exchange Rate | 51 |
| | Evaluations of IMF - World Bank Programme | 55 |
| 2 | **Method of Optimal Control** | 57 |
| | Deterministic Control | 57 |
| | Deterministic Control Using Pseudo-Inverse | 60 |
| | Stochastic Simulations | 62 |
| | Stochastic Control with Additive Stochastic Process | 65 |
| | Case of Certainty Equivalence | 68 |
| | Stochastic Control with Learning (Adaptive Control) | 69 |
| | Stochastic Optimal Control Solution | 69 |
| | Updating Method of Reduced-form Coefficients and their Covariance Matrices | 71 |
| | Derivation of the Filter | 73 |
| | Stability | 77 |
| | Controllability | 78 |

| | | |
|---|---|---|
| 3 | **Recent Advances in Macroeconomic Policy Analysis and the Analytical Structure of the Control Model** | 81 |
| | Responses of Monetary and Fiscal Policies under Alternative Expectation Structures: Mathieson Model | 82 |
| | Monetary Policy: Adjustment under Adaptive Expectations | 84 |
| | Fiscal Policy: Adjustment under Adaptive Expectations | 85 |
| | Rules Versus Discretion | 88 |
| | Proximate Targets | 89 |
| | Fiscal Instruments: Interrelations with Monetary Instruments | 91 |
| | Fiscal Rules and Intertemporal Budget Constraint | 93 |
| | Policy Models for Growth and Adjustment | 95 |
| | Alternative Policy Analysis: Analytical Structure of the Econometric Model | 98 |
| 4 | **Estimation and Analysis of the Model** | 105 |
| | Estimations | 107 |
| | Explanation of an Equation Structure | 109 |
| | Dynamic Properties of the Model | 110 |
| | Response Multiplier | 111 |
| | Dynamics of Response Multipliers | 112 |
| | Monetary Dynamics | 116 |
| | Fiscal Dynamics | 116 |
| 5 | **Analysis of the Result of the Control System** | 117 |
| | Analysis over the History: 1977-1985 | 122 |
| | Future Planning: 1988-1996 | 134 |
| | Concluding Comments | 142 |
| | Bibliography | 143 |
| | Index | 149 |

# List of Figures

| | | |
|---|---|---|
| Figure 1.1 | GDP and Domestic Demand India | 3 |
| Figure 1.2 | Consumer Prices - India | 4 |
| Figure 1.3 | Current Account Balance and as Percentage of GDP - India | 5 |
| Figure 1.4 | Goods Exports Vs Good Imports - India | 6 |
| Figure 1.5 | Investment and Savings - India | 7 |
| Figure 1.6 | Medium and Long Term Debt (as Percentage of GDP) - India | 8 |
| Figure 1.7 | Source of Medium and Long Term Debt - India | 9 |
| Figure 1.8 | Debt Service Ratio - India | 10 |
| Figure 1.9 | Asia External Debt Outstanding | 11 |
| Figure 1.10 | Real Exchange Rate Indicies - India | 12 |
| Figure 1.11 | Gross Domestic Product - Chile | 53 |
| Figure 1.12 | GDP and Domestic Demand - Chile | 54 |
| Figure 1.13 | Annual CPI Inflation - Chile | 54 |
| Figure 1.14 | Foreign Debt a Percent of GDP - Chile | 54 |
| Figure 1.15 | Current Account Balance - Chile | 54 |
| Figure 3.1 | Monetary Policy; Adjustment under Rational Expectation | 83 |
| Figure 3.2 | Fiscal Policy; Adjustments under Rational Expectation | 85 |
| Figure 3.3 | Adjustment under Adaaptive Expectation | 86 |
| Figure 3.4 | Adjustment under Adaaptive Expectation | 87 |
| Figure 3.5 | Comparison of Rational and Adaptive Expectations | 87 |
| Figure 5.1 | Domestic Absorption | 127 |
| Figure 5.2 | Price Level | 127 |
| Figure 5.3 | Newly Created Money Stock | 131 |
| Figure 5.4 | Net Domestic Asset Creation | 131 |
| Figure 5.5 | Governement Expenditure | 132 |
| Figure 5.6 | Tax Revenues | 133 |

# List of Tables

| | | |
|---|---|---|
| Table 1.1 | India's Economic Scene: Growth Performance | 13 |
| Table 1.2 | Growth Rate Net Domestic Product | 14 |
| Table 1.3 | Growth Rate of Industry | 19 |
| Table 1.4 | Average Capital Output Ratio | 20 |
| Table 1.5 | Rate of Growth of Capital, Net Domestic Product and Technology | 21 |
| Table 1.6 | Net Domestic Product and Capital Formation | 21 |
| Table 1.7 | Money Supply, Price and National Income, 1950-1951 to 1955-1956 | 23 |
| Table 1.8 | Financial Policies 1950-1951 to 1955-1956 | 24 |
| Table 1.9 | Money Supply, Price and National Income, 1956-1957 to 1960-1961 | 24 |
| Table 1.10 | Financial Policies, 1956-1957 to 1960-1961 | 25 |
| Table 1.11 | Banking Policies 1950-1961 | 25 |
| Table 1.12 | Money Supply, Price and National Income, 1960-1967 | 26 |
| Table 1.13 | Financial Policies, 1960-1967 | 27 |
| Table 1.14 | Banking Policies 1960-1967 | 27 |
| Table 1.15 | Money Supply, Price and National Income, 1969-1970 to 1973-1974 | 28 |
| Table 1.16 | Financial Policies, 1970-1974 | 29 |
| Table 1.17 | Banking Policies 1970-1974 | 29 |
| Table 1.18 | Money Supply, Price and National Income, 1974-1978 | 30 |
| Table 1.19 | Financial Policies, 1974-1978 | 30 |
| Table 1.20 | Banking Policies 1974-1978 | 31 |

| | | |
|---|---|---|
| Table 1.21 | Money Supply, Price and National Income, 1978-1985 | 32 |
| Table 1.22 | Financial Policies, 1980-1985 | 32 |
| Table 1.23 | Banking Policies 1980-1985 | 33 |
| Table 1.24 | Some Important Ratios 1980-1989 | 34 |
| Table 1.25 | Banking Policies 1985-1990 | 35 |
| Table 1.26 | Money Supply, GNP and Price Level 1985-1990 | 35 |
| Table 1.27 | Financial Policies 1985-1989 | 35 |
| Table 1.28 | Comparative Export Performances | 39 |
| Table 1.29 | Exchange Rate and Balance of Payments | 40 |
| Table 1.30 | Relative Price Indicies of Exports | 41 |
| Table 1.31 | Domestic Resource Cost, Effective Rate of Protection and the Rate of Profit 1980-1981 | 41 |
| Table 1.32 | Comparative Growth Rates of Asian Countries (real GNP) | 42 |
| Table 1.33 | Comparative Export Performances: India and China | 33 |
| Table 1.34 | Nominal Exchange Rate, Real Exchange Rate and Real Export Growth | 43 |
| Table 1.35 | Foreign Debt - India | 44 |
| Table 1.36 | Medium and Long Term Debt -- India | 46 |
| Table 1.37 | Nominal and Real Effective Exchange Rates | 50 |
| Table 4.1 | Real Characteristic Roots of the Model | 111 |
| Table 4.2 | Response Multiplier and Endogenous Variables | 112 |
| Table 4.3 | Response Multipliers | 113 |
| Table 4.4 | Monetary Dynamics, Fiscal Dynamics | 115 |
| Table 5.1 | Historical Path 1978-1986 | 118 |
| Table 5.2 | Target Paths | 119 |
| Table 5.3 | Optimal Adaptive Control Path | 120 |
| Table 5.4 | Optimal Stochastic Control Paths | 121 |
| Table 5.5 | Target Paths | 127 |
| Table 5.7 | Optimal Paths: Experiment 1 | 128 |
| Table 5.7 | Optimal Paths: Experiment 2 | 129 |
| Table 5.8 | Foreign Debt: Experiment 1 | 141 |
| Table 5.9 | Underlying Assumptions on Debt Services | 141 |

# Preface

The main task of this book is to analyze India's economic scene in a consistent manner and develop a system to derive adaptive control solutions. In order to introduce the subject which is not so familiar to the economist we need to go through some analysis regarding the developments of various techniques of control system and the relevant macroeconomics. The purpose is not to forecast but provide an alternative to the so called 'market system' which has since 1991, flooded out any mention of the word 'planning'. I do not think 'planning' is dead, in fact a quick comparison between India's performance since 1991 will show even the overall performances at the macro level is not any better than what was achieved when planning was in operation. The micro level performances in India and in other developing countries who were going through the transitional process from 'semi-planned' or 'mixed planned' system to a complete 'marked-economy' are much worse, although these are beyond the scope of this book.

The method used in this book was developed as a joint work of myself and Alexis Lazaridis without whose support I would not be able to complete the book. The support of Professor Thomas Kronsjo in the psychological sphere has provided the stimulus. The academic atmosphere of the University of Kent was also very helpful.

Dipak R. Basu
*Canterbury*
*January 1995.*

# 1 India's economic scene and the behaviour of the monetary–financial instruments

**Introduction**

Forty years ago, India's dream was to create a 'socialistic pattern' of society through planning in a mixed economy and to achieve a reasonable standard of living. Today that dream is yet to be fulfilled. India with its annual per capita income of $290 falls into the World Bank's lower category of developing country. South Korea is twice as rich and even China has enjoyed three times as rapid growth of per capital national product. The poor economic performance is fully reflected in other aspects. More than a third of India's population of 300 million people subsist below the official poverty line. This implies basic nutritional needs are not met.

However, compared to its historical past, it did well. Between 1900 and 1946, India experienced total stagnation; GNP grew more slowly than population, food production virtually stood still and the result was extreme hardship and poverty. During the postwar years, the rate of growth was about 3-5 per cent per year but there are problems. The share of manufacturing in total national product has remained static at around 16 per cent since the mid 1960s. In South Korea and China, by contrast, the share of manufacturing in GNP has climbed to 28 per cent and 37 per cent respectively. Even in agriculture, India's performance has been relatively unimpressive despite the 'green revolution'. Buffer stocks in grain have piled up in recent years but only because people are too poor to buy. Productivity in some crops has risen, but the gains are unevenly spaced and outshone by the achievements of other countries.

The question is: What went wrong? Population growth seems a convenient scapegoat. However, even if India's population had stagnated since 1947, per capita income would only be around $500, which is chronically low by the standards of successful developing countries. Population growth is not something intrinsically beyond human control.

One may draw attention to the macro economic policies pursued by India. However, by the standards of most developing countries and many industrialised countries for that matter, India has followed extremely responsible macro economic policies. There was no hyper inflation or debt crisis (until recently). The volatility of growth rates has largely reflected the natural instability of agricultural output. At times macro policy may have been wrongly cautious. Micro economic policy, on the other hand, has been inconsistent. The planners until very recently took little notice of price mechanism. By the late 1970s, industry was handicapped by an array of bureaucratic controls. Companies were unable to open factories, expand capacity, alter their product mix or close without explicit government approval and this usually involved long delays and negotiations with numerous different ministries.

Foreign trade had performed in a strange way. Imports were seen as a threat to the goal of self reliance. Only imports deemed essential to India's domestic development were allowed. At the same time, the export sector was ignored or discouraged through taxation. When other East-Asian countries grew rich through export, India stood on the side-line.

However, since 1985, a new wind of change was blowing. The last Prime Minister, Rajib Gandhi, had tried to introduce a new line of thought to liberalise the economy in 1985. Although during the late eighties the pace towards liberalization was stopped, somehow due to some serious external development, India has now no choice but to opt for a liberalised economy. The 'Gulf War' has particularly destroyed India's growing market in the countries such as Iraq, Kuwait and Saudi Arabia. At the same time, the remittances sent by the Indians working in various Arabian Gulf countries shrank to a very low level. The Soviet Union which used to be the major backer and financier for India's international sector (defence industries in particular, and the oil and petrochemical sector), has disappeared from the world scene as a major economic power. As a result, India has no choice but to resort to the IMF induced adjustment programme, i.e. to go away from the centrally planned economy to a market driven economy where monetary-fiscal policies instead of physical planning will rule the future. The purpose of the research is to explore that possibility given the fact that India will resist most strongly any attempt by the international agencies to discard the planning system which provides a rudimentary protection for socially deprived people and protects jobs. It is thus realistic to assume that much liberalization will take place in the private industrial sector to remove bureaucratic obstacles, but planning at least for the public sector will remain. In the core sector of the economy, the public sector will continue to play a dominant role, exports will be encouraged, but imports will be restricted due to a shortage of foreign exchange. Given that scenario, the question is what role the monetary-financial and exchange rate policies can play. The subsequent chapters are an attempt to provide the answers.

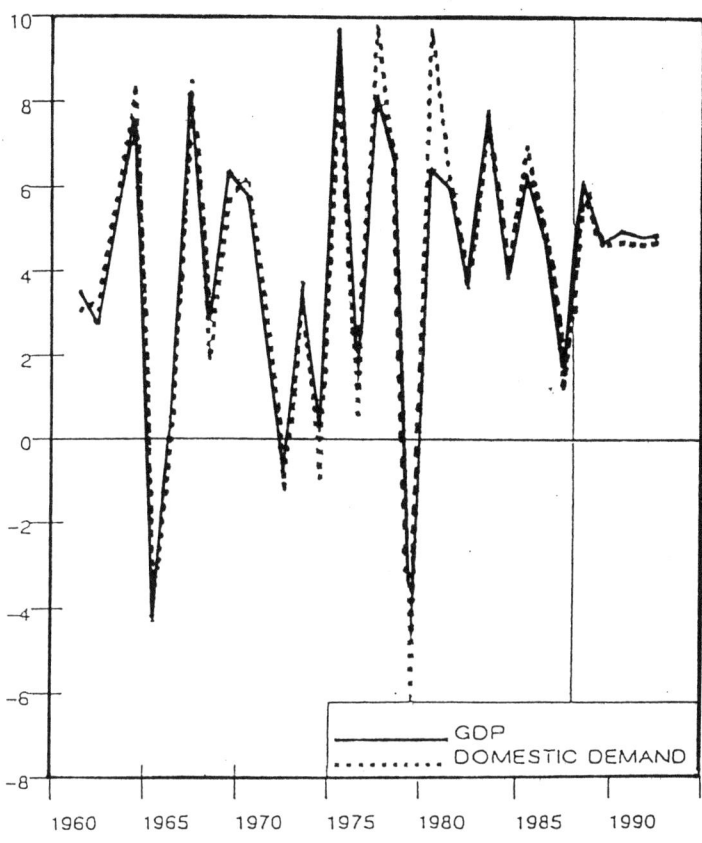

**Figure 1.1** GDP and Domestic Demand – India (% change from a year ago)

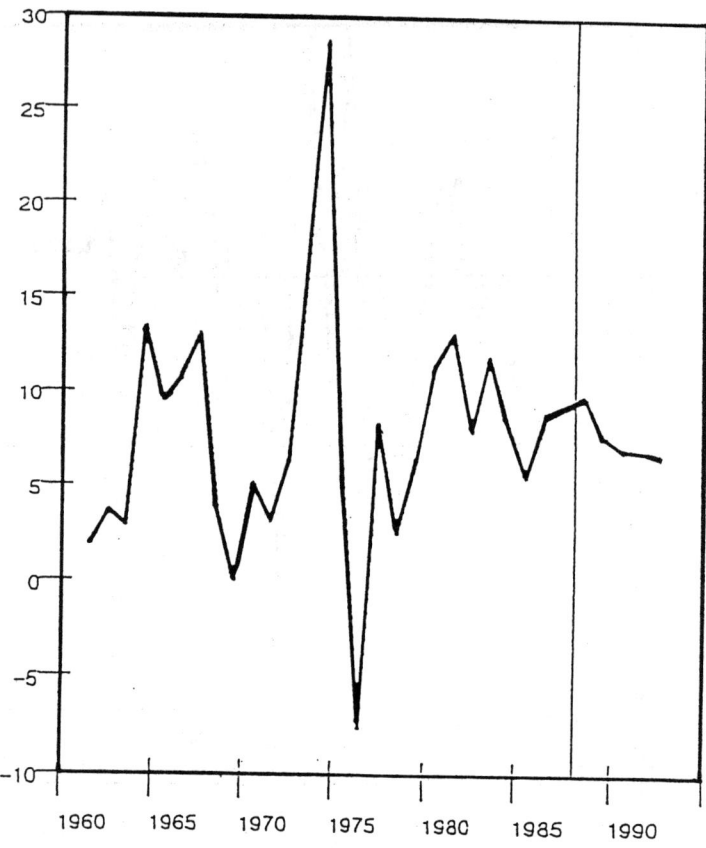

**Figure 1.2 Consumer Prices – India (% change from a year ago)**

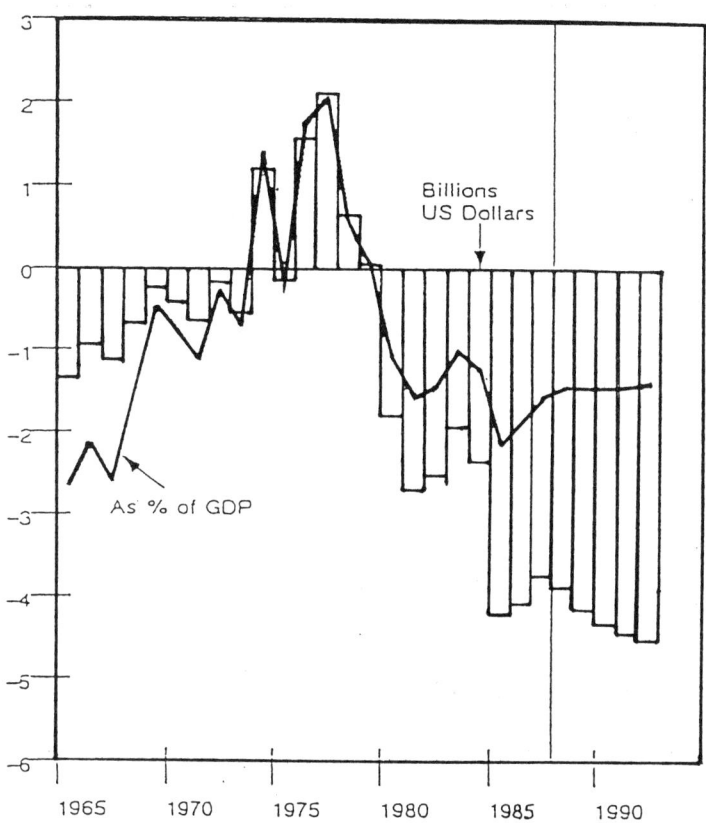

**Figure 1.3 Current Account Balance and as % of GDP – India (Billions of U.S. dollars)**

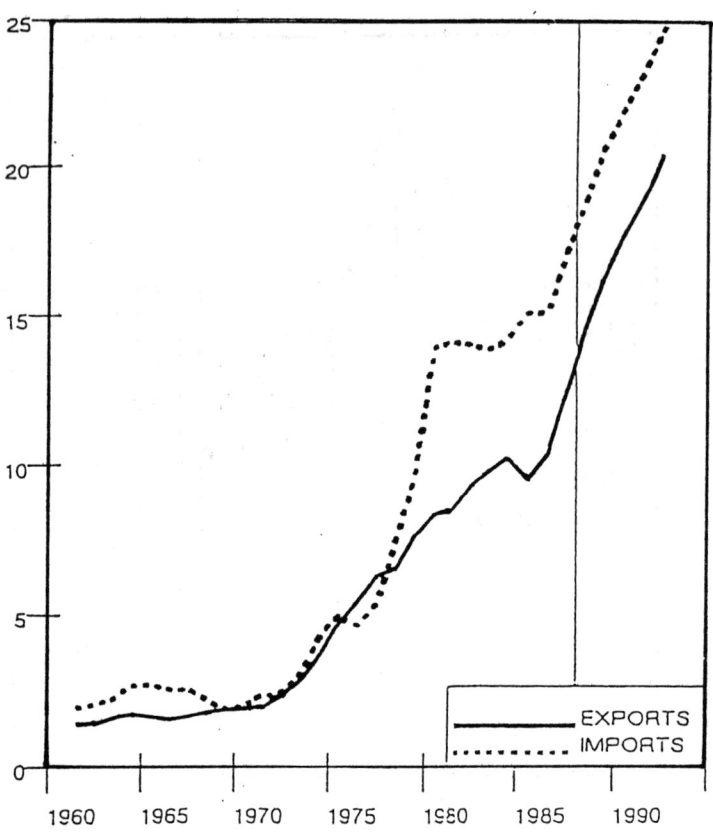

**Figure 1.4** Goods Exports Vs Good Imports – India (billions of U.S. dollars)

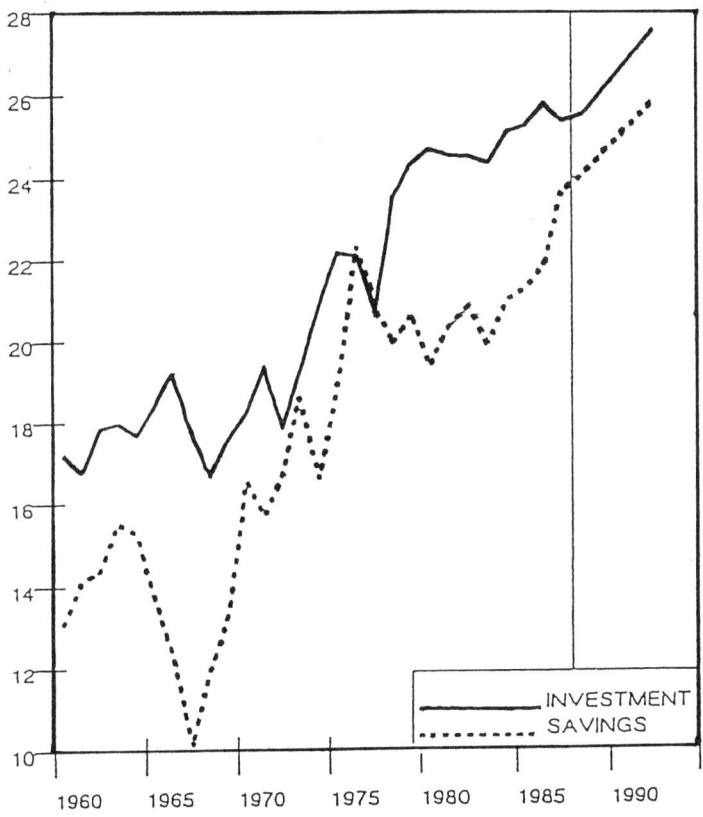

**Figure 1.5 Investment and Savings – India (as % of GDP)**

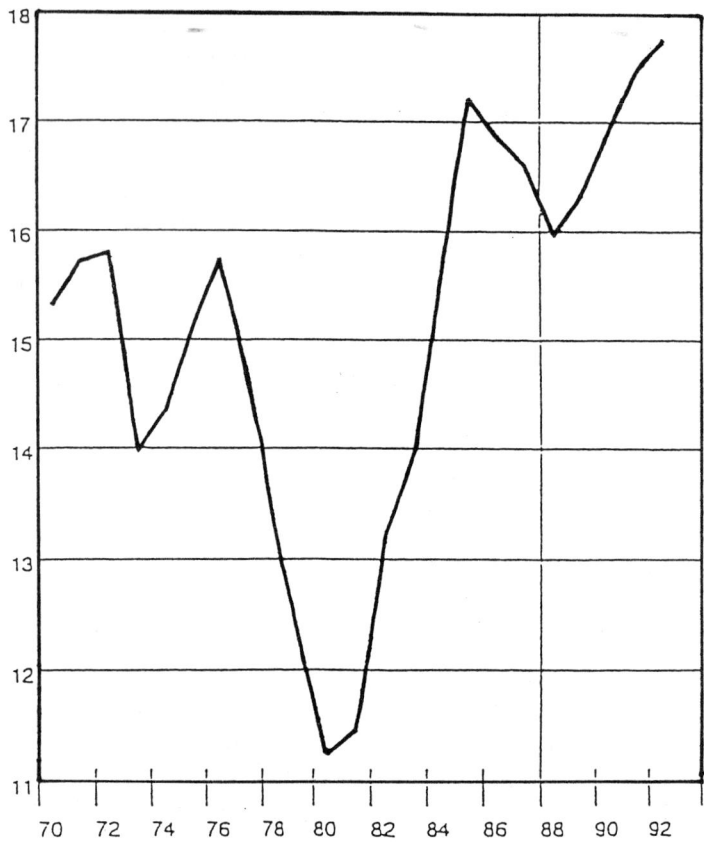

**Figure 1.6 Medium and Long Term Debt – India (as % of GDP)**

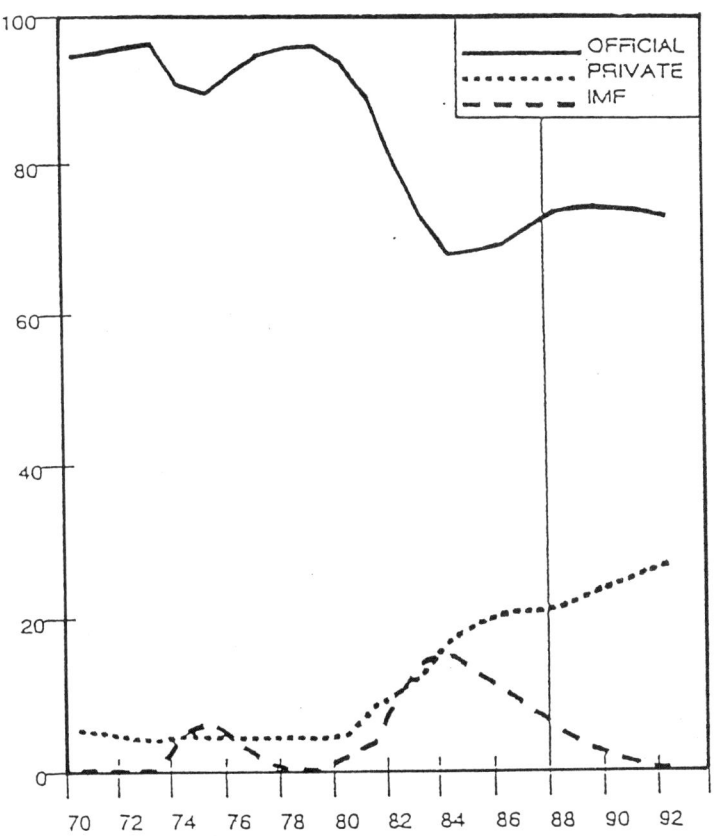

**Figure 1.7** Source of Medium and Long Term Debt – India (as % of total debt)

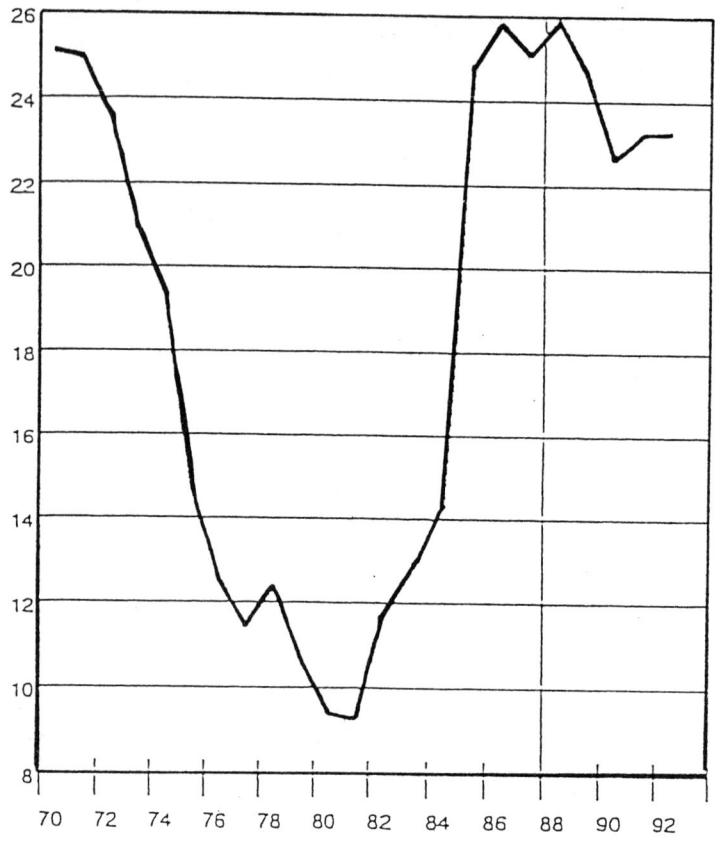

**Figure 1.8 Debt Service Ratio – India (medium and long term debt, incl. IMF)**

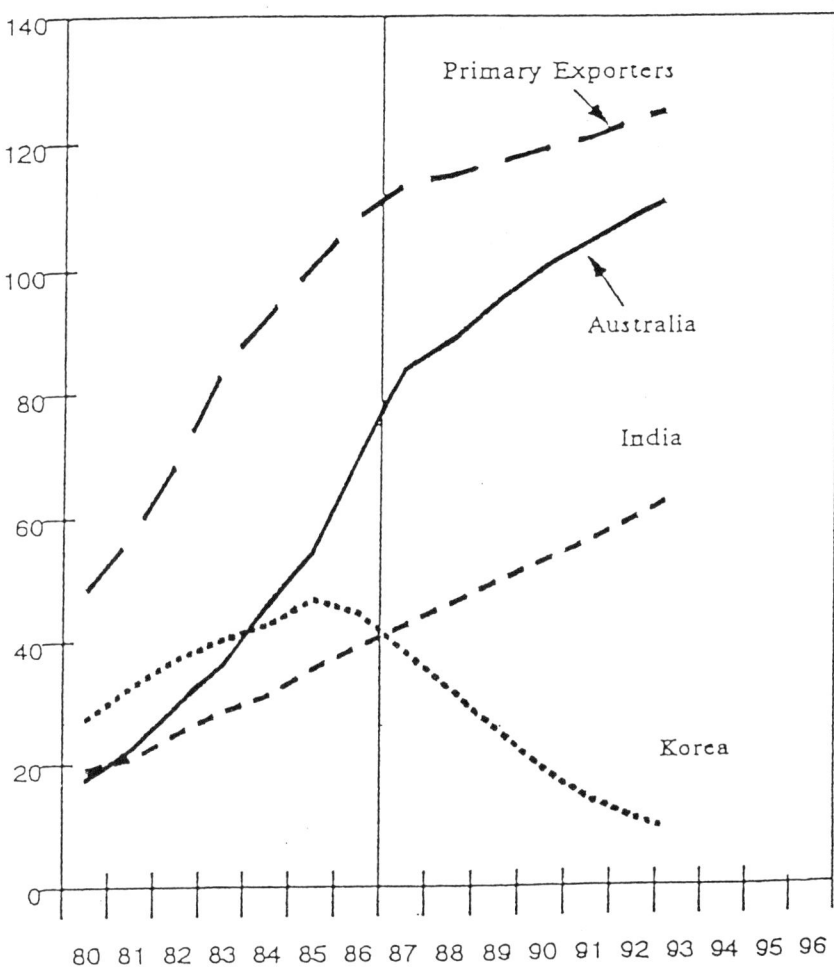

**Figure 1.9 Asia External Debt Outstanding (billions of U.S. dollars)**

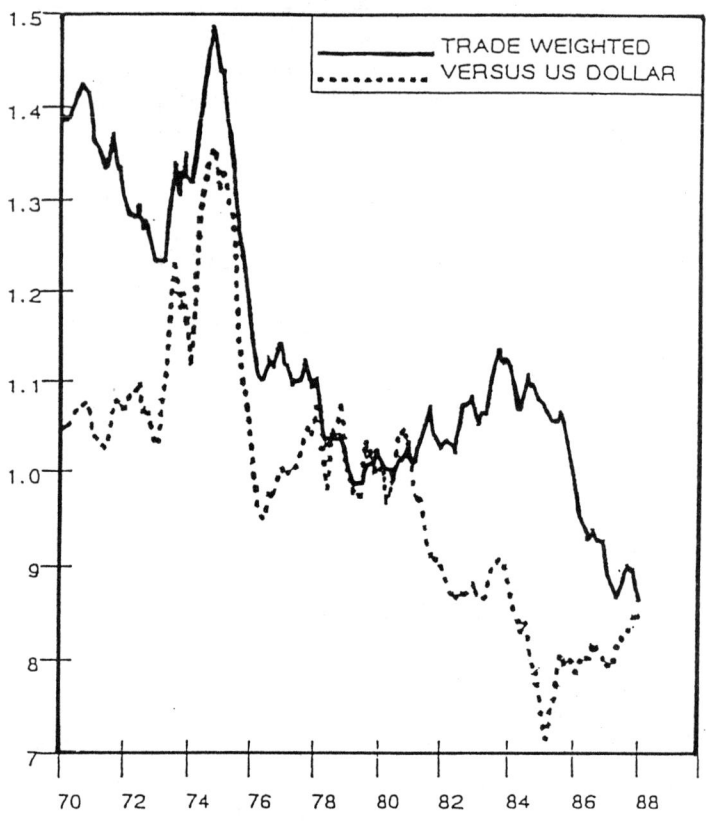

**Figure 1.10 Real Exchange Rate Indices – India (rise = appreciation of rupee)**

**Table 1.1**
**India's economic scene: growth performances**

| % p.a. real terms | 1950 to 1973 | 1973 to 1985 | 1950 to 1985 |
|---|---|---|---|
| GDP | 3.53 | 4.25 | 3.63 |
| GDP[1] | 3.41 | 3.84 | 3.44 |
| Primary Sector | 2.13 | 2.44 | 2.25 |
| Secondary Sector | 5.82 | 4.46 | 5.02 |
| Tertiary Sector | 4.71 | 6.18 | 4.94 |

Source: CSO, India
1 Excluding public administration and defence.

India started its five year plan in 1951 with the Soviet Union as a model. Although India was not a socialist country and most parts of the economy were in private hands (which include the agricultural sector, the most dominant part of the economy), it was conceived that the private sector alone could not pull up the economy from the pathetic economic situation that prevailed at that time with the large refugee problem, stagnated economy and backward agricultural country. The description fitted the Soviet Union in 1918 as well, and the dramatic transformation of the Soviet economy into an advanced industrialised state within two decades had provided India with the perfect example to follow. The Mahalanobis model (Mahalanobis, 1953) had provided the theoretical justification for a Soviet style economic planning where maximization of growth potentials can be achieved through massive investments in the capital goods producing sector i.e. heavy industry, steel, chemicals etc. Although there was no effort to mobilise primary sources of surplus (i.e. agricultural surplus) as the Soviet Union did, in India through the '1956 Industrial Policy', extensive series of licence, quotas and permit systems were arranged to control output, investment, location and direction of the private sector's efforts. In the comparative tranquil period of the first and second plans, India's performances were not far behind its targets, in fact it had excelled targets during the first plan.

## Table 1.2

### Growth net domestic product (1970-71 Price)

|  | target | achievement | gap |
|---|---|---|---|
| First five year plan | 3.2 | 3.4 | 1.1 |
| Second five year plan | 4.5 | 3.7 | -0.8 |
| Third five year plan | 6.0 | 3.6 | -2.4 |
| Fourth five year plan | 5.1 | 3.2 | -1.9 |
| Five five year plan | 5.0 | 3.9 | -1.1 |

Source: Five-year Plan Progress reports, Planning Commission.

Disaster struck India during the 1960s. The Chinese invasion of 1962 and subsequently Pakistan's Invasion in 1965 had destroyed the certainty of the old conception that India did not have to worry about defence and it could spend all her resources on development. Defence expenditure as a percentage of GDP rose from 2% before 1962 to 4% between 1962 and 1972. Foreign aid to India was suspended as well. That was followed by a severe drought in 1966 and as a result of that, India had to surrender to the IMF and accept a massive devaluation of the rupee in 1966. However, the devaluation could not achieve its goal, (see Bhagwati and Srinivasan 1975); because of the IMF pressures development plans were suspended as well; good fortune came in the form of the green revolution when between 1967 and 1971 net cereal production rose by 50%. At the same time in 1969, the Coal Industry and major Commercial Banks were nationalised to pave the way for a dramatic increase in the extension of the banking services to the rural areas and to the poorer section of the people. Along with agriculture, both GDP and Industrial production had recovered. However, the response of the government at that time was to reduce public investment and as a result recovery was slow. The positive aspects of the economy during 1970-71 in terms of higher than expected rate of growth of GDP (5.6%) and good harvests were evaporated by the massive influx of refugees from Bangladesh followed by the war with Pakistan. As a result, public expenditure rose at the rate of 22%. At the same time in 1972, agricultural production fell. The government had resorted to deficit financing and the money supply rose rapidly. The result was a runaway inflation of about 25% in 1972-73.

That was not all. 1973-74 had also experienced the 'Oil Price Shock' and as a result there was inflation and recession in most parts of the developed world and India could not escape the consequences. India in 1974 was spending about 75% of its export earnings only to import crude oil, the balance of payments deficit went up to 9.6 billion rupees in 1974-75 from a surplus of 280 million rupees in 1972-73. According to Balassa (1984), India had lost about 2.1% of its GNP during the period 1974-76 due to the oil price shock.

However, the crisis brought about by the oil producing countries had mixed blessings. A large and very lucrative market in the Middle East countries was opened up for India's export. A large number of Indian companies were getting contracts in the construction industry throughout the Middle East and as a result a large number of people from India had obtained jobs there. The combined effects of higher export earnings, remittances by the companies and Indian workers in the Middle East had created a surplus in the balance of payments accounts for the period between 1976-1981. From 1974 to 1976, exports rose by 60% (39% in volume) and imports by 18% (nil in volume). Although some (Joshi and Little, 1987) may attribute this to the fall in the real exchange rate by about 17%, the true cause was the sudden increase in demands in the Middle East, which the Western countries could not satisfy in the short term. As India was self-sufficient regarding industrial production, due to the geographical proximity it was the obvious choice for importers. However, due to the lack of dynamism in the Indian industry as a consequence of bureaucratic controls, very soon Korea, China and other East Asian countries had taken over that market.

Due to the balance of payments surplus imports were liberalised to some extents, however money supply (M3) grew at a rate of 20% between 1975-78, mainly to finance administration because capital expenditure remained the same between 1975-78. However, danger was lurking behind. The second Oil Price Shock in 1979 had affected India quite badly. Between 1978-1980, the balance of payments was affected adversely by 4.3 billion rupees. The adverse affect on the GDP was about 3% (Balassa and McCarthy, 1984) for the period 1978-79; the current account deficit was about 2 billion rupees for that period. As a proportion of exports the deficit was about 20%, and unlike during the first 'Oil Price Shock', export could not expand rapidly. On top of that, agricultural production fell by 15% in 1979-80 and the prices rose by 17% in 1979-80 and by 18% in 1980-81. The reaction of the government was to reduce public spending and money supply. However, imports particularly of capital goods and defence went up sharply when exports were really stagnant mainly due to the world recession. The international political situation was not conducive either. After the Soviet involvement in Afghanistan in 1979, Pakistan was receiving massive arms aid from the USA and several Middle Eastern countries. In order to match that, India had to import massive amounts of defence related equipment and within a short time, India had become one of the most important defence importers of the world. The result of that on the balance of payments was quite severe and India had to resort to commercial borrowing, the consequences of which we can see in recent years when debt service to export had reached 40% in 1988 (about 38% in 1991) whereas the Debt to GDP ratio had reached 17% in 1988 (about 18% in 1991) which is alarming by any standards.

The 1985 budget initiated a new direction in Indian foreign trade policies. Import controls were relaxed and simplified and exporters received massive import concessions. The new trade policy was designed to liberalise the economy in general to initiate a more 'outward oriented' economic regime. However, continuous sluggishness of exports and the growing deficit in the balance of payments weakened the 'modernization' process of the Indian economic system. Consensus emerged (Lucas 1989) that liberalization of trade alone could not rescue the economy, what was needed was the wholesale reform of the industrial policy thus liberating private sectors from bureaucratic controls. The structure of industrial controls under revision had since 1956 relied upon industrial licensing, price ceilings and import quotas as well as minimum wages, employment laws, excise and profit taxes, export incentives and duties to direct the pattern of industrial development (a detailed explanation is provided later). Despite substantial public sector industrial investment, by the early 1980s the private sector continued to generate some 75% of both value added and employment in manufacturing. The recent budget of 1991 has addressed that issue: a large number of industries are now de-licensed, import policies are further liberalised and the economy is moving towards a market system. A detailed analysis regarding the background to this new economic policy is given in a later section.

### Banking policies and credit controls

It is essential to describe the banking regulations in India in order to understand the monetary scene.

While the Reserve Bank of India was set up in 1935 primarily for the purpose of securing monetary stability and operating the credit system of the country to its advantage, the various provisions of the Indian Companies Act were introduced for the safeguard of the interest of shareholders of limited companies. Although deposits received from the public constitute the main resources and working capital for a banking company, there are no specific provisions in either of the two enactments which would ensure the safety of the depositors' money in a banking company. With a view to plugging these loop holes, the Banking Companies Act of 1949 was introduced. In order to ensure that a banking company is in a position to pay its depositors in full as and when their claims accrue, the provisions of section 24 of the Act make it obligatory for every banking company to maintain a certain percentage of its assets in liquid form. It was originally stipulated that every banking company would be required to maintain in cash, gold or unencumbered approved securities an amount which shall not, at the close of day, be less than 20% of its total time and demand deposits. The above liquidity ratio, i.e. the statutory liquidity ratio, was increased in successive stages to 35% in 1981.

Under section 42 of the Reserve Bank of India Act, 1934, every scheduled bank in India is required to maintain an average daily balance of 3% of its demand and time deposits. This reserve ratio which stands at 7%, can be increased to the maximum of 15%. With the nationalization of 20 major Commercial Banks (in addition to the State Bank of India), a statutory liquidity requirement may not be necessary as a safety measure. However, the Reserve Bank is using it as an instrument of credit control. The Commercial Banks can keep their liquid assets in the form of cash or gold or government securities. No Bank will keep any idle cash or gold with it except for its day to day use. Obviously the choice should be the government's securities. A Commercial Bank is now required to invest at least 30 to 32% of its funds to government securities yielding low returns ranging between 3% to 9%. A bank is entitled to interest from the Reserve Bank of India on the balance in excess of the minimum of 3% of its liabilities. A Banking Company is now required to deploy at least 40% of its credit priority and neglected sectors and it is required to lend at least 1% of its total advances under Differential Rate of Interest Scheme at a concessional rate of interest of 4%. Interest rate is determined by the Reserve Bank of India through its discount rate at which other Commercial Banks can borrow and by direct instructions to the Commercial Bank as these are within the public sector. However, recently proposals made so as to relax these types of control over the Commercial Banks, rather the Reserve Bank will specify a minimum lending rate in the same fashion as the Bank of England.

Banks however, have not been the principle source of long term finance in India. This role has been left to the specialised development finance institutions operating at both state and federal level. According to the Industrial Development Bank of India (IDBI) for the year 1988-89, assistance sanctioned and distributed by all the financial institutions recorded an average annual growth of 24.8% and 23.8% during the 1980s. The financial institutions viz IDBI, Industrial Finance Corporation (IFC), Industrial Credit and Investment Corporation (ICIC), Life Insurance Corporation (LIC), Unit Trust of India (UTI), and General Insurance Corporation (GIC) accounted for 83.4% of total sanctions of all financial institutions for 1988-89 against 77.2% in 1987-88. The Industrial Reconstruction Bank of India concentrates on 'Sick Industries'. In practice, financial institutions are a large interlocking network with IDBI having share-holdings in several of the other large institutions as well as in many state bodies providing them with finance. UTI, LIC and GIC are closely involved as purchasers of the debt of the institutions. Their lending policy has been monolithic. Loans have been arranged through consortia, with no question of competition for business. Recently steps are being taken to introduce more competition in the raising of funds by the institutions themselves.

## Industrial policy and licensing systems

Without understanding India's industrial policy a lot of misunderstanding may emerge. Because of the ranges of licences, quotas, permits regarding investment, production, expansion or location it was not possible for the private sector which provides about 78% of India's value added to invest according to their plans or to respond to the demand of traditional cost factors, most important of all, interest rate. As a result traditional investment functions to determine the reaction of the industrial sector in response to changes in policies is not applicable for India.

India happens to be among the few countries in the world with an extensive industrial licensing system. It was started with the Industrial Policy Resolution in 1948 which was amended in 1956 to implement the 'Mahalanobis' model of Indian planning where emphasis was on heavy and machine-building industries, expansion of the private sector, encouragement of the cooperative sector and diffusion of ownership and management in the private sector.

Two schedules were introduced. The first includes 17 industries ranging from atomic energy and air transport to generation and distribution of electricity. Only the public sector is allowed to operate in some areas. The second schedule includes 12 industries where the private sector is expected to cooperate and supplement the public sector. The list comprises fertiliser, chemicals, pulp, road and sea transport. The remaining industries are left with the private sector. Small scale and ancillary units are exempted from licensing. Undertakings popularly known as large industrial houses attract the provisions of the Monopolies and Restricted Trade Practices Act and the Foreign Exchange Regulation Act. They have to get clearance from the appropriate authorities for setting up new units or expanding existing ones. In 1975 and 1976 attempts were made to liberalise the industrial policy. That had allowed full utilization of installed capacity of 29 industries and automatic expansion at the rate of 25 per cent in five years. In addition, diversification within the licensed capacity was permitted for a wide range of industries. In 1982, the government had relaxed the licensing policy and the constraints on capacity utilization. The core sector industries, hitherto prohibited for the private sector were thrown open to large houses as well as the FERA companies. These new groups of industries added to the list are high technology production equipment carbon products, high pressure pipes, rubber and printing machinery.

It was claimed that liberalization would stimulate growth and import substitutions and promote economies of scale and adoption of high technology. In the same vain, import policy has changed in 1985 to allow imports of capital goods. Recent changes in the industrial policy in 1991 (discussed in a later section in more detail) is intended to remove irritants of clearances and bureaucratic inertia. The controls so far have not promoted priority industries and MRTP law has not stopped the growth of large houses. Trusted licensing systems have provided a protected market placing a premium on inefficiency.

The performance of the industrial sector is mixed. India has achieved near self sufficiency regarding the ranges of industrial products and the technological advancements have been highly impressive, particularly in the public sector. The strength of India's industrial sector was, in fact, responsible for the reversal of fortune for India immediately after the first oil price shock of 1974, when India had turned its chronic balance of payments deficits into surpluses by exporting most types of industrial products to the new market of oil producing countries. However, considering the investments made so far, the performances are not that impressive (Lucas, 1988).

Table 1.3
growth rate of industry (per cent per annum)

| years | | | rate of growth of net value added |
|---|---|---|---|
| 1955-56 | to | 1965-66 | 6.5 * |
| 1965-66 | to | 1975-76 | 3.5 * |
| 1975-76 | to | 1980-81 | 4.5 * |
| 1980-81 | to | 1983-84 | 6.2 * |
| 1984 | to | 1985 | 8.6 |
| 1985 | to | 1986 | 8.7 |
| 1986 | to | 1987 | 9.1 |
| 1987 | to | 1988 | 7.3 |
| 1988 | to | 1989 | 8.7 |
| 1989 | to | 1990 | 8.6 |
| 1990 | to | 1991 | 8.4 |
| 1991 | to | 1992 | 0.5 |
| 1992 | to | 1993 | 2.3 |
| 1993 | to | 1994 | 3.0 |

Note: * Compound growth rate
Source: National Accounts Statistics.

Growth rate fell during the 1960s mainly due to acute financial problems and again during the early 1980s due to the second oil price shock when India could not adjust quickly. However, the industrial growth since the mid 1980s is satisfactory, due to a liberalised atmosphere. The sudden collapse of industrial growth in 1991 is due to the demise of the Soviet Union and the Gulf war which led to severe foreign exchange problems.

The causes of slower industrial growth are (a) bureaucratic stranglehold over the industries (as a result Indian industries are very slow to respond); (b) inadequate infrastructure and inadequate supplies of power; (c) bias against exports. Due to export pessimism built into the planning methodology of India, domestic industries were protected from international competitions and, at the same time, import control and self sufficiencies in industry were the goal of the planners. Although India has achieved self sufficiency (Lucas 1989) by reducing import content in production and consumption drastically, India could not take advantage of the dramatic growth of the world trade in post-war years. The result is that the industrial sector depends on domestic resources only (foreign investment was discouraged by the industrial policy of 1956 due to its many restrictions). Lack of international finance and international demand had reduced the potential growth of the industrial sector. At the same time, the trade protection and licensing system (which, in practice, gives monopoly power for some producers over the domestic market, due to the corruption which is endemic in the political system) makes home sale more profitable than exports. The net result of slower rate of growth of output along with increasing investments in the public sector financed by budget deficits implies increasing capital output ratio, which is a common feature in many planned economies (Hazra, 1985: Gomulka, 1976). Hazra (1985) and Rao (1983) have calculated that the capital output ratio went up from 2.5 during 1950-54 to 4.23 during 1975-79 and to 4.80 in 1980-81. The net domestic saving as a proportion of net domestic product increased from 7% during the 1950s to about 20% during the late 1970s.

### Table 1.4
### Average capital output ratio

| period | capital output ratio (Rao) | capital output ratio (Hazra) | index 1950-54 = 100 |
| --- | --- | --- | --- |
| 1950-54 | 2.50 | 2.45 | 100.0 |
| 1954-59 | 2.71 | 2.73 | 108.4 |
| 1960-61 | 2.92 | 3.04 | 116.8 |
| 1965-69 | 3.43 | 3.40 | 137.2 |
| 1970-74 | 3.88 | 3.79 | 155.2 |
| 1975-79 | 4.20 | 4.23 | 168.0 |
| 1979-80 | 4.58 | 4.62 | 183.2 |
| 1980-81 | 4.80* | 4.72 | 192.1 |

* Estimated by Hazra

Source: Hazra (1986), Rao (1983).

There is also evidence that several countries had accumulated capital much faster than India.

**Table 1.5**
**Rate of growth of capital, net domestic product (NDP) and technology**

| country | time period | growth of capital | growth of NDP | growth of technology* |
|---|---|---|---|---|
| Japan | 1952-71 | 6.00 | 6.14 | 3.6 |
| USA | 1960-73 | 4.00 | 4.30 | 1.3 |
| Germany | 1950-60 | 6.90 | 8.20 | 4.7 |
| USSR | 1927-67 | 6.50 | 5.25 | 1.8 |
| China | 1952-80 | 5.80 | 5.00 | 0.5 |
| Brazil | 1950-70 | 4.14 | 6.20 | 2.8 |
| Mexico | 1950-70 | 5.90 | 0.07 | 2.0 |
| Argentina | 1950-70 | 3.20 | 3.50 | 1.4 |
| Chile | 1950-70 | 3.60 | 3.90 | 1.2 |
| India | 1950-80 | 4.70 | 3.50 | 0.7 |

* Total Factor Productivity
Source: Hazra (1986), Brahamananda (1981).

The above table shows that for only a few countries, e.g. India, China, USSR and Mexico, the growth of capital is greater than the growth of NDP and a higher rate of growth of technology implies a higher rate of growth of NDP. Although India's saving rate is high and as a result the rate of investment is high, the rate of absorption of technology is low by international standards. As a result, capital has become increasingly inefficient. From the table, we can see that both the private and the public sector are demonstrating this feature.

**Table 1.6**
**Net domestic product and capital formation :**
**public and private sector (at constant 1970-71 prices)**

| year | all public sector | | | (Rs billion) | |
|---|---|---|---|---|---|
| | NDP | NDCF | ΣNDCF | NDP/ΣNDCF | DP/NDCF |
| 1950-51 | 12.72 | 5.57 | 5.57 | 2.28 | 2.28 |
| 1960-61 | 25.44 | 14.37 | 121.24 | 0.21 | 1.76(.35)* |
| 1970-71 | 50.07 | 23.24 | 343.44 | 0.14(.11)* | 2.15(1.78)* |
| 1978-79 | 91.72 | 43.96 | 616.07 | 0.15(.11)* | 2.08(1.10)* |

* Figures in the brackets are for the public sector manufacturing industries.

| year | all private sector | | | | |
|---|---|---|---|---|---|
| | NDP | NDCF | ΣNDCF | NDP/ΣNDCF | NDP/NDCF |
| 1950-51 | 156.01 | 15.42 | 15.42 | 10.11 | 10.11 |
| 1960-61 | 213.11 | 13.87 | 129.91 | 1.64 | 15.36(.26)* |
| 1970-71 | 295.12 | 28.03 | 338.76 | 0.87(.39)* | 10.53(3.92)* |
| 1978-79 | 374.42 | 41.52 | 609.63 | 0.61(.41)* | 9.01(7.31)* |

\* Figures in brackets are for the private corporate sector.
Source: National Accounts Statistics, CSO and Hazra (1982).

NOTE: (a) NCP = Net Domestic Product; NDCF = Net Domestic Capital formation

Considering the NDP/NCDCF which is considered to be the incremental output/Capital ratio, the private sector is comparatively more efficient than the public sector. That is certainly a drain in resources, as it accounts for half of India's fixed capital formation. Recent economic policies are aiming to reduce these inefficiencies by privatising at least some sections of the public sector and giving more autonomy to the public sector companies.

**Monetary and financial policies**

In India monetary and fiscal policies are interlinked. Given the planned and non planned expenditure the government tries to raise the money either by taxation, or by borrowing from the Reserve Bank of India and from other financial institutions in return for government securities. It can also raise money from profits of the public sector. The deficit which cannot be financed in this way has to be financed either by foreign borrowing (and aid if there is any) or by direct money creation by the Reserve Bank of India. The Reserve Bank also has complete control on the net foreign exchange reserves due to complete exchange controls. Thus the deficit in the annual budget can be reflected in the increase in money supply quite easily. At the same time government bond sales to the Reserve Bank of India may add to the volume of high powered money as the Reserve Bank got to finance its purchases of government bond in some way, particularly when due to the absence of any bond market the rates of return on government bonds are very low. The Reserve Bank can control the commercial banks currency to reserve ratios which determine liquidity positions of the commercial banks and control the circulation of credit and thereby money supply. Another instrument is the ratio of reserve to deposit in the commercial banks. The Central discount rates of the Reserve Bank of India (the rate at which the commercial banks will borrow from the Reserve Bank of India) can be used as an instrument when the

Commercial banks need to borrow money from the Reserve Bank of India although it is not used as such. Instead interest rates charged by the commercial banks are determined directly by the government and the Reserve Bank of India. In addition to this the commercial banks are subjected to selective credit controls from time to time for specific loans advanced in order to reduce speculative reactions in the market for commodities and food grain in particular.

This analysis of monetary policy in India ultimately boils down to the analysis of budget deficits and money supply and their effect on the price levels and growth. Budget deficit certainly increases money supplies and thereby price level, however, reductions in the budget may lead to reductions in planned investment expenditures (as it is difficult if not impossible to reduce public consumption expenditures without reducing subsidies which can be politically unrealistic) and future growth of GDP thus creating pressure on price levels.

*First five year plan (1951-1956)*

India's industrial development had started with the first five year plan against a background of acute shortages of food and raw materials in general and rehabilitation problems of millions of refugees after the partition of the country. Money supply during the plan period rose by 10%, however, the wholesale price index declined by 13% due to 18% increase in national product.

Table 1.7
Money supply, price and national income 1950-51 to 1955-56
(annual % charges)

| years | money supply | GNP * | price level |
|---|---|---|---|
| 1950-51 | 0.6 | 2.82 | 10.4 |
| 1951-52 | 0.6 | 3.95 | 2.1 |
| 1952-53 | -6.5 | 6.02 | -12.4 |
| 1953-54 | 0.7 | 2.49 | 4.6 |
| 1954-55 | 4.8 | 1.94 | -6.9 |
| 1955-56 | 10.7 | 4.96 | -5.0 |

Source: Report on Currency and Finance, RBI.
* (Constant 1948 price).

## Table 1.8
### Financial policy 1950-51 to 1955-56 - (Rs billion)

|  | public expenditure | tax revenue | deficit | domestic borrowings | foreign borrowings | foreign aid |
|---|---|---|---|---|---|---|
| 1950-51 | 4.36 | 4.71 | -1.15 | .24 | .03- | -- |
| 1955-56 | 6.76 | 5.84 | -3.51 | 2.78 | -- | .38 |

Source: International Financial Statistics IMF.

Deficit went up to RS 3.52 billion on 1955-56. The deficit was financed by increased taxation and domestic borrowing. This period is characterised by price stability, high industrial and agricultural growth despite evidence of inflationary financing through budget deficits.

*Second five year plan 1956-57 to 1960-61*

Second five year plan was a bold attempt to industrialise the country through massive investment in heavy industry and import control measures.

## Table 1.9
### Money supply, price and national income 1956-57 to 1960-61
### (annual % charge)

| years | money supply | GNP | price level |
|---|---|---|---|
| 1956-57 | 8.5 | 4.96 | 13.8* |
| 1957-58 | 5.0 | -1.00 | 2.9 |
| 1958-59 | 2.4 | 6.97 | 4.2 |
| 1959-60 | 6.7 | 1.80 | 3.7 |
| 1960-61 | 6.8 | 7.33 | 6.6 |

* constant 1948 price
Source: Report on Currency and Finance, RBI.

## Table 1.10
### Financial policy, 1956-57 to 1960-61
### (Rs billion)

|  | public expenditure | tax revenue | budget deficit | domestic borrowing | foreign borrowing | foreign aid |
|---|---|---|---|---|---|---|
| 1956-57 | 11.84 | 8.0 | -6.77 | 5.88 | .74 | .15 |
| 1957-58 | 12.50 | 7.93 | -7.34 | 4.94 | 2.04 | .18 |
| 1958-59 | 11.18 | 9.13 | -6.97 | 5.34 | 1.59 | .38 |
| 1959-60 | 13.12 | 10.35 | -6.49 | 3.78 | 2.18 | .30 |
| 1960-61 | 14.37 | 12.39 | -6.03 | 3.23 | 2.51 | .34 |

Source: International Financial Statistics, IMF.

Compared to the first plan, the rate of growth of GNP is high along with higher rate of growth of money supply and price level. We can see a clear link between deficit financing, money supply and price level. Public expenditure rose along with domestic and foreign borrowing. The Planning Commission has anticipated that the deficit financing would create inflation and it had recommended quantitative as well as qualitative controls on credit as an important brake on the effects of deficit financing; a deficit financing would lead to the addition to the money supply which would lead to secondary expansion of credit by the Commercial bank. In this regard, we can analyse the banking policies during that important phase of Indian planning where the seeds of industrial development were planted.

## Table 1.11
### Banking policies 1950-61

| year | reserve/deposit | currency/deposit | credit/deposit |
|---|---|---|---|
| 1950 | .12 | .12 | .55 |
| 1955 | .10 | .10 | .65 |
| 1957 | .08 | .09 | .73 |
| 1958 | .07 | .08 | .64 |
| 1959 | .06 | .07 | .62 |
| 1960 | .08 | .10 | .72 |
| 1961 | .08 | .09 | .81 |

Source: IMF.

As one can see, reserve ratio has declined during the early part of the plan and during the latter part it went up, however it could not arrest the growth of credit. The currency to deposit ratio stayed more or less constant over the second plan, but credit to deposit ratio had improved. The deposit went up due to expansion of the banking system. Due to the combined efforts of budget deficit, monetary growth and credit expansion, the rate of inflation went up from 2.29% in 1957 to 6.6% in 1960. However, that was the period of growth for the economy. In fact, the credit to deposit ratio was rather low for an expanding economy. In a similar period the credit to deposit ratio in Japan was almost unity.

*The third plan (1961-62 to 1965-66)*

The Third Plan has experienced extreme difficulties in terms of adverse agricultural seasons, Chinese invasion in 1962 and Pakistan's invasion of 1965 and total suspension of foreign aid in the later part of the plan. The plan has started with the same objectives as that of the Second plan i.e. to industrialise at a rapid rate but there were danger signals in the price front in the beginning. As a result monetary and financial policies were designed to suppress further inflationary pressures on the economy. Although total public deficit was designed to 7.3% of total public outlay, at the end it was 13.3% due to the difficulties the economy had faced in terms of expansion of defence expenditures.

### Table 1.12
### Money supply price and national income 1960-67
### (annual % charge)

| year | money supply | GNP. * | GDP * | price level |
|---|---|---|---|---|
| 1960-61 | 6.8 | 3.02 | 2.56 | 6.6 |
| 1961-62 | 4.4 | 2.32 | 2.78 | 0.2 |
| 1962-63 | 8.9 | 6.94 | 5.33 | 2.2 |
| 1963-64 | 12.0 | 6.55 | 7.05 | 5.8 |
| 1964-65 | 8.7 | -4.63 | -4.30 | 12.8 |
| 1965-66 | 11.1 | -6.26 | 1.12 | 8.1 |
| 1966-67 | 9.2 | 16.71 | 8.15 | 15.9 |

* (In constant 1980 prices)
Source: Report on Currency and Finance, RBI and IMF.

## Table 1.13
### Financial policy 1960-67
### (Rs billion)

| | public expenditure | tax revenue | budget deficit | domestic borrowing | foreign borrowing | foreign aid |
|---|---|---|---|---|---|---|
| 1960-61 | 14.37 | 12.39 | -6.03 | 3.23 | 2.51 | .34 |
| 1961-62 | 18.57 | 14.87 | -8.75 | 5.07 | 3.20 | .66 |
| 1962-63 | 23.89 | 19.00 | -10.94 | 6.59 | 3.74 | .71 |
| 1963-64 | 25.37 | 20.27 | -11.71 | 4.62 | 5.18 | 1.31 |
| 1964-65 | 26.55 | 23.84 | -12.39 | 7.32 | 4.82 | .68 |
| 1965-66 | 30.38 | 25.29 | -17.21 | 9.95 | 7.04 | .84 |
| 1966-67 | 31.46 | 25.45 | -14.60 | 8.00 | 6.01 | .18 |

Source: IMF.

Price inflation was quite alarming, particularly at the end of the plan period. Money supply had expanded along with increased budget benefit. Although tax revenue was increased substantially during this time, it was not enough due to increased public expenditure. The result was increasing volume of domestic and foreign borrowings.

## Table 1.14
### Banking policies, 1960-67

| year | revenue/deposit | currency/deposit | credit/deposit |
|---|---|---|---|
| 1960 | .08 | .10 | .72 |
| 1961 | .08 | .09 | .81 |
| 1962 | .06 | .07 | .84 |
| 1963 | .06 | .07 | .88 |
| 1964 | .06 | .07 | .86 |
| 1965 | .07 | .08 | .87 |
| 1966 | .07 | .08 | .87 |
| 1967 | .07 | .07 | .87 |

Source: IMF.

The banking policies during that period were designed to control inflationary pressures on the economy. Revenue to deposit ratio was declined in 1962 due to income and public expenditures. and in particular, defence expenditures. Currency to deposit ratio also went down whereas the credit to deposit ratio went up due to increased public expenditure. There is a close and positive relationship between private investment and public expenditure, so despite the inflationary pressure, that period was a period of expansion.

However, during the later half of the period, both reserve to deposit ratio and the currency to deposit ratio went up to combat extraordinary economic crisis due to failure of the agricultural sector and war in 1965 which had caused serious inflationary pressures.

*Fourth plan (1968-70 to 1973-74)*

The apparent failure of the third plan over the price front led to the serious economic crisis in 1965; as a result, India had to accept IMF's economic conditions. The Rupee was devalued in 1965 which had the result of further inflationary pressures, with no real gain to the trade sector. However, due to IMF pressures, five-year plans were abandoned for four years and were replaced by annual plans. Due to liberalised credit policy during that period, there was a significant increase in bank credit to the private sector, however, inflation was contained by the so-called 'Green Revolution' in 1967-68. At the same time public expenditure was reduced along with the budget deficit. The fourth plan was designed to reduce the inflationary pressure and to create a condition of stability. However, for reasons beyond the control of the government, the budget deficit and money supply rate was significantly higher than expected. The war with Pakistan in 1971 and the cost of rehabilitation of refugees had nearly bankrupted the government. On the top of that, the first 'Oil Crisis' of 1974 had created an extraordinary economic crisis.

**Table 1.15**
**Money supply, prices and national income 1969-70 to 1973-74**
**(annual % charges)**

|  | GNP.* | money supply | price level |
|---|---|---|---|
| 1968-70 | 6.4 | 10.5 | 3.7 |
| 1970-71 | 6.0 | 11.8 | 5.5 |
| 1971-72 | 1.1 | 14.0 | 5.6 |
| 1972-73 | 1.3 | 15.7 | 10.6 |
| 1973-74 | 5.7 | 15.2 | 20.2 |
| Annual Average | 3.5 | 13.4 | 8.9 |

* at 1960-61 prices
Source: Reserve Bank of India.

The real output had a very low rate of growth in 1971-73. At the same time, the money supply went up due to huge expansions of public expenditure (which was basically unproductive expenditure on defence). Rates of inflation were quite high for those years. The sudden increase in the rate of inflation in 1973-74 was due to the combination of a bad agricultural season and the imported inflation as a result of the first 'Oil Crisis' in 1973-74, when oil prices were increased suddenly and as a result transport costs throughout India went up creating an inflationary spiral.

### Table 1.16
### Financial policies 1970 to 1974
### (Rs billion)

|      | public expenditure | tax revenue | budget deficit | domestic borrowing | foreign borrowing | foreign aid |
|------|--------------------|-------------|----------------|--------------------|-------------------|-------------|
| 1970 | 39.26              | 33.28       | -13.55         | 10.59              | 3.32              | .38         |
| 1971 | 49.32              | 40.56       | -16.00         | 10.62              | 3.46              | .22         |
| 1972 | 55.19              | 45.73       | -21.76         | 19.44              | 2.93              | .25         |
| 1973 | 58.11              | 49.69       | -16.98         | -3.29              | 4.65              | 16.74       |
| 1974 | 73.68              | 62.46       | -24.64         | 17.14              | 7.05              | 1.04        |

Source: IMF.

Public expenditure went out of control after 1971. Although tax revenues were increased at a healthy rate, it was not enough. The result was a very high level of deficit which fed the money supply. Both foreign and domestic debts were increased at the same time in the absence of foreign aid during 1968-73.

### Table 1.17
### Banking policies 1970 to 1974

| year | reserve/ deposit | currency deposit | credit deposit |
|------|------------------|------------------|----------------|
| 1970 | .06              | .07              | .90            |
| 1971 | .06              | .07              | .88            |
| 1972 | .06              | .07              | .83            |
| 1973 | .09              | .09              | .85            |
| 1974 | .07              | .07              | .85            |

Source: IMF.

As we can see from the above table, reserve ratio was used in 1973 to reduce the inflationary spiral. At the same time, currency to deposit ratio of the banking system was increased. The result was that the credit to deposit ratio had declined. However, during the fourth plan, increase in money supply was substantially higher than the increase in real output and the annual average rate of increase in the wholesale price was close to the difference between average annual rate of growth on money supply and the real income.

*Fifth plan (1974-75 to 1977-78)*

The fifth plan had inherited a severe economic crisis with inflation running at a rate of 2.5% per month during 1974-75. Anti-inflation policies had dominated the planning the budget deficits and monetary expansions were in the package of measures taken to control inflation. Anti-inflationary policies were those of reduction of public expenditure, wage rate, domestic credit expansion and money supply. Money supply was increased at a rate of 6.92% in 1974-75 (15.2% in 1973-74). However, the result was a much lower rate of growth of GNP which was reduced from 5.7% in 1973-74 to 1.02% in 1974-75.

### Table 1.18
### Money supply, price and national income
### (annual % charge)

| year | money supply | GNP* | price level |
|---|---|---|---|
| 1974-75 | 6.92 | 1.02 | 25.00 |
| 1975-76 | 11.27 | 9.16 | 1.09 |
| 1976-77 | 20.26 | 1.37 | 2.08 |
| 1977-78 | 14.71 | 7.43 | 5.21 |
| Annual Average | 13.79 | 4.75 | 7.85 |

* In constant 1970-71 price
Source: Reserve Bank of India.

### Table 1.19
### Financial policies 1974-78
### (Rs billion)

| | public expenditure | tax revenue | budget deficit | domestic borrowing | foreign borrowing | foreign aid |
|---|---|---|---|---|---|---|
| 1974 | 73.68 | 62.46 | -24.64 | 17.14 | 7.05 | 1.04 |
| 1975 | 90.59 | 74.71 | -34.80 | 21.58 | 15.19 | 2.83 |
| 1976 | 100.53 | 84.52 | -39.58 | 20.77 | 11.37 | 2.71 |
| 1977 | 112.65 | 94.29 | -41.16 | 57.77 | 4.34 | 3.22 |
| 1978 | 129.70 | 108.54 | -53.45 | 20.81 | 4.81 | 2.67 |

Source: IMF.

## Table 1.20
## Banking policies

| year | revenue/deposit | currency/deposit | credit deposit |
|---|---|---|---|
| 1974 | .07 | .07 | .85 |
| 1975 | .06 | .06 | .89 |
| 1976 | .06 | .07 | .89 |
| 1977 | .10 | .09 | .84 |
| 1978 | .10 | .11 | .80 |

Source: IMF.

Despite the policy objectives of the plan, money supply was expanded at the same rate as in the previous plan and the rate of inflation was reduced due to a good agricultural season, not really due to any banking policies which were out of line with anti-inflationary policies; budget deficit was not reduced either. However, due to increased national income, inflationary pressure was reduced significantly, in fact, overall growth rate for GNP was 4.75 which was higher than that in the previous plan.

Both domestic and foreign borrowings were expanded at a very high rate. The banking policies however were quite conservative. Reserve ratio currency ratio went up and credit ratio went down, thus creating a credit squeeze in the economy mainly to reduce excessive money supply due to increasing budget deficits. At the same time public borrowing went up at an alarming rate. One significant part of the increased money supply was the expansion of foreign exchange in flows, which went up from Rs 2.38 billion in 1974-75 to Rs 14.63 billion in 1976, due to remittances from the Middle East. At the same time, time-deposits were increased along with increased deposit rate. Another significant aspect of this period was the government's borrowing for the Reserve Bank of India.

*Sixth plan (1980-1985)*

After two annual plans between 1978 to 1980, the fifth plan was introduced in 1980 when the Indian economy was in a healthy condition. The growth rate of the economy (i.e. GNP) was 7.7% in 1980-81. However, money supply rate was high as well, along with a slightly higher rate of inflation. During 1978-79, the money supply rate was 21.9% and as a result inflation rate was 12.2%, the money supply rate was reduced a little in the subsequent period, however it was always quite excessive compared to the rate of growth of GNP. As a result, inflationary pressures were always there, only to be contained by sudden improvements in the agricultural sector. Because of increased productivity of the economy, the rate of growth of the GNP was higher in this period and the inflation rate was manageable.

### Table 1.21
### Money supply, GNP. and price level 1978-1985
### (annual % charge)

| year | money supply | GNP. | price level |
|---|---|---|---|
| 1978-79 | 21.9 | 5.9 | 12.2 |
| 1979-80 | 18.7 | 4.8 | 2.1 |
| 1980-81 | 18.1 | 7.7 | 5.9 |
| 1981-82 | 12.5 | 4.6 | 10.1 |
| 1982-83 | 16.1 | 1.7 | 6.6 |
| 1984-85 | 15.4 | 5.4 | 5.6 |
| Annual Average 1980-85 | 16.1 | 5.4 | 7.2 |

Source: Reserve Bank of India.

### Table 1.22
### Financial policies 1980-85
### (Rs billion)

| year | public expenditure | tax revenue | budget deficit | domestic borrowing | doreign borrowing | foreign aid |
|---|---|---|---|---|---|---|
| 1980 | 167.02 | 121.11 | -92.99 | 77.58 | 12.82 | 4.36 |
| 1981 | 198.62 | 149.46 | -91.16 | 72.94 | 9.68 | 3.84 |
| 1982 | 237.89 | 175.42 | -111.32 | 132.40 | 12.54 | 3.98 |
| 1983 | 287.20 | 255.02 | -133.03 | 85.5 | 12.09 | 3.76 |
| 1984 | 351.32 | 296.01 | -175.08 | 161.05 | 13.08 | 4.17 |
| 1985 | 430.07 | 361.02 | -222.05 | 208.09 | 13.07 | --- |

Source: IMF.

However, as we can see from the financial analysis, India had entered into a different mood that someone might describe as a 'Brazil' syndrome of high spending, high level of borrowing and monetary expansion which may create initial high rate of growth as India had experienced during the 1980s but at the same time it has created a situation of long-term financial crisis. The total amount of budget deficit during 1980-85 was Rs 827.07 billion which is about 35% of the GNP in 1985 (at current price in 1985). Similarly the total amount of domestic borrowing during that period is about 31% of the GNP in 1985. Total domestic debt has reached Rs 1083.6 billion in 1985 which is again 46% of the GNP in 1985. One may agree that domestic borrowing cannot cause alarm, because the present generation will pay to the future generations the amount it had borrowed. However, if the public borrowings are not going to be invested in the productive public sector, if instead public borrowings are meant to supplement government consumption (i.e. administrative expenses) and defence expenditures, very soon the economy will be within the 'Ricardo Equivalence' (Barro, 1974) trap i.e. in future the government will need to increase taxation in order to repay the public borrowings. As Minhas (1986) has observed during the eighties, there was no relationship between the deficit financing and the growth rate, what was expected if the deficit financing is meant for public investment. This was due to increased defence expenditure during the 1980s. The defence expenditure was about Rs 2.5 billion in 1961-62. In 1987-88 it has reached about Rs 125.1 billion. Although defence expenditure may be considered to be unproductive, a recent example of China shows it can be highly productive in terms of export earnings of defence equipment.

Table 1.23
Banking policies

| year | reserve/deposit | currency/deposit | credit/deposit |
|---|---|---|---|
| 1980 | .12 | .12 | .79 |
| 1981 | .12 | .12 | .80 |
| 1982 | .13 | .13 | .81 |
| 1983 | .12 | .12 | .81 |
| 1984 | .11 | .12 | .80 |
| 1985 | .14 | .15 | .79 |

Source: IMF.

If we compare Banking policies of this plan to that of the previous plan (1974-1978), we can see very easily the reserve ratio was used very strictly in order to combat inflationary surges in 1978-1979 and in 1981-1982 which were both due to external factors. The impact of the higher reserve ratio and the currency to deposit ratio was in terms of lower inflation rate in the following year but at the cost of lower rate of growth of the economy. The average reserve ratio and credit to deposit ratio was .12 and .8 respectively. The overall effect of this strict monetary policies was reflected in the average price inflation and the average rates of growth of GNP. The average price inflation rates for this plan and the previous plan were 7.2 and 7.8 respectively, whereas the average rate of growth of the GNP were 5.4 and 4.7 respectively. However, we tend to remember that the average money supply rate for the current plan was 16.1 compared to 13.8 in the previous plan, so it is quite clear that strict monetary policies had their desired effect on inflation. The average credit to deposit ratio for this plan was .80 compared to .85 in the previous plan. The lower rate of credit expansion to the private sector was neutralised by the expansion of the public sector, high rate of growth of private financial inflows from abroad and good agricultural seasons. The respectable rate of growth of the economy perhaps has created over optimism on the part of the policy makers which has resulted in higher rates of borrowing both domestic and foreign on the expectation that higher productivity growth can pay off the loans. However, that expectation was not fulfilled in the way it was expected.

*Seventh plan (1985-90)*

Following the apparent success of the sixth plan financed by debt, the government was in an optimistic situation during the seventh plan to continue their policies of borrowing from both domestic and foreign sources with the premise that a budget deficit can expand the economy and in the medium term can finance itself. As a result, money supply was expanded on 1985, 1987 and in 1988. The result was price inflation reaching almost 9%, which was damped down due to domestic growth. The rate of growth of the GNP was quite respectable for the most part of this period.

### Table 1.24
### Some important ratios

| year | budget deficit/ GNP | domestic debt/ GNP | domestic borrowing/ public expenditure | tax revenue/ GNP | public exp./ GNP |
| --- | --- | --- | --- | --- | --- |
| 1980 | .072 | .379 | .46 | .094 | .131 |
| 1981 | .061 | .378 | .48 | .101 | .134 |
| 1982 | .168 | .437 | .55 | .107 | .145 |
| 1983 | .071 | .409 | .28 | .104 | .146 |
| 1984 | .076 | .387 | .40 | .129 | .153 |
| 1985 | .085 | .416 | .48 | .137 | .165 |
| 1986 | .093 | .453 | .49 | .143 | .178 |
| 1987 | .084 | .464 | .41 | .144 | .180 |
| 1988 | .084 | .459 | .43 | .140 | .178 |
| 1989 | .066 | .474 | .34 | .153 | .174 |

Source: IMF.

## Table 1.25
## Banking policies

| year | reserve/deposit | currency/deposit | credit/deposit |
|---|---|---|---|
| 1985 | .148 | .154 | .79 |
| 1986 | .135 | .159 | .78 |
| 1987 | .159 | .164 | .75 |
| 1988 | .163 | .165 | .74 |
| 1989 | .160 | .166 | .75 |
| 1990 | .152 | .166 | .73 |

Source: IMF.

## Table 1.26
## Money supply, GNP* and price level 1985-90
(annual % charges)

| year | money supply | GNP | price level |
|---|---|---|---|
| 1984-85 | 15.40 | 5.4 | 5.6 |
| 1985-86 | 16.07 | 2.3 | 8.7 |
| 1986-87 | 13.47 | 4.5 | 8.8 |
| 1987-88 | 16.49 | 8.7 | 9.4 |
| 1988-89 | 18.03 | 5.6 | 6.2 |
| 1989-90 | 11.34 | 4.9 | 8.7 |

Source: Reserve Bank of India and IMF; * at constant 1990 prices.

## Table 1.27
## Financial policies 1985-89
(Rs billion)

| year | public expenditure | tax revenue | budget deficit | domestic borrowing | foreign borrowing |
|---|---|---|---|---|---|
| 1985 | 430.7 | 361.2 | -222.5 | 208.9 | 13.7 |
| 1986 | 518.1 | 420.7 | -272.0 | 258.5 | 19.4 |
| 1987 | 597.1 | 480.8 | -278.8 | 244.4 | 32.7 |
| 1988 | 700.6 | 554.6 | -330.9 | 300.9 | 25.1 |
| 1989 | 769.8 | 675.8 | -292.3 | 262.5 | 29.9 |

Source: IMF.

The significant feature during this period was the new policy initiative taken in 1985. Imports were relaxed along with wide ranges of domestic industrial licensing restrictions which had initiated a new era of liberalization of the private sector. The private sector had responded vigorously, although commercial banking policies were not conducive to this new liberalization. As one can see from the banking policy, reserve ratios were kept high (along with currency to deposit ratio). The result is that the credit to deposit ratio has declined over the period from .79 in 1985 to .73 in 1990. That implies the emphasis was still on the public sector and the public expenditure as a proportion of the GNP went up from .13 in 1980 to .18 in 1987. This expansion of the public expenditure was financed by domestic borrowing along with foreign borrowing. Domestic debt as a percentage of GNP rose from .37 in 1980 to .47 in 1989. Considering the fact that only a minority of people in India are going to hold government stocks and bonds, an increasing percentage of the GNP is going to be controlled by a minority of stock holders with serious implications for inequalities of income for future generations.

Efforts were made to increase tax revenues and tax revenues as a ratio of GNP went up from .09 to .15 from 1980 to 1989 but at the same time public expenditure as a ratio of GNP went up from .13 in 1980 to .18 in 1987 and a large part of these expenditures are due to defence which unlike that in China may not add anything to India's future export earnings. The general impression one may get is that although policy objective of the government was to promote the private sector, monetary policies (particularly banking policies) were not geared to that objective. At the same time financial policies indicate an increasing share of the government in the national economy and as these were financed by borrowing the future growth prospective of the economy can be restricted by the increased tax rates which will be needed to finance that high level of public borrowing, unless we can see any serious improvement in the productivity of the public sector. The result was that at the end of the decade the so called liberalization was only restricted to the import liberalization with the pace of liberalization of the domestic private sector being somehow depressed. Recently Lucas (1989) has demonstrated that trade liberalization without corresponding removal of restrictions on the private sectors offers little gains. That is the reason why the new economic policy initiatives were introduced in 1991 to liberalise the private sector, which are analysed below.

**Foreign trade, exchange rate and debt**

India immediately after the independence from colonial rule wanted to develop an independent economic system so as not to rely upon the vagaries of the world economic orders still dominated by the old colonial powers. The model was that of the Soviet Union. The method it thought most appropriate was a process towards import substitution so that they would have to import only the very essentials. In order to achieve that, India has implemented a variety of measures to restrict imports; tariffs, quotas, total restrictions on imports of certain items and domestic investment policies geared to the production of most importables. That has affected exports in two different ways. The direct impact of the investment bias towards import substitution leads to neglect of the export industries. The indirect effect came from the incentives given to the domestic firms towards the production of import substitutables. Import taxes raise the price of the importable and thus it is more profitable for the domestic firms to produce import substitutables rather than exportables.

At the same time there are some built-in constraints for the domestic firms in a developing country like India to export. Marketing systems for their exports are virtually non existent, in view of the fact exports are expensive and are considered to be uncertain prospect for the domestic firms. At the same time the government itself suffers from export pessimisms. It is worried about the uncertainties of the world economy and considers export earnings are an insecure source of public revenues. Also it is assumed that exports are facing inelastic demand in the world market. As a result exports are considered to be residual. However subsequent economic pressures are altering that attitude.

India like every other developing country went through the painful experience of massive deficits in the balance of payments and temporary stoppage of the industrial development process. In the early 1950s, India with comfortable surplus in the balance of payments had a liberal import regime during its first plan (1951-56). However, in the beginning of the second plan (1956-61) along with its drive for industrialization and import substitution, foreign exchange crisis has become acute. The war with China in 1962 and with Pakistan in 1965 led to a crisis in India's balance of payments, as a result of which the rupee was devaluated in 1966, there was a temporary stoppage of the development plan and exchange rate became flexible. India's trade policy had to be modified giving way to import liberalization and export promotions. However 'green revolution' that followed in 1967 and onwards in India's agricultural sector has made India 'self-sufficient' in food thereby lifting a major burden for India's balance of payments i.e. cost of food imports. However the continuation of factors like the refugee problem and the war with Pakistan in 1971, bad agricultural seasons in 1973-74 and finally the 'oil crisis' of 1974 led to a critical situation in the balance of payments in 1974 when India had to spend almost two thirds of its export revenue just to meet the import cost of crude oil. However the 'oil crisis' of 1974 had opened up a new avenue for Indian exports i.e. exports of consumer goods and particularly services to the Middle East. The upsurge of export revenue and foreign exchange inflows had resulted in comfortable surpluses in the balance of payments during the late 1970s. This surplus of the balance of payments had helped India to overcome the second 'oil crisis' of 1981. Thus despite stagnant exports throughout the 1980s, India's import levels were not reduced. However, due to the reduction in the price of crude oil in the world market, a number of Middle Eastern countries since 1985 have started reducing their current expenditure on development. The result was a serious decline of earning of foreign exchange from the Middle East for India and as a result India's balance of payments has started deteriorating since then and foreign debt is increasing year by year. However the main problem is the lack of growth of exports.

Recent export performances of India are nothing but dismal. India's economy is two and a half times the size of Korea and yet its merchandise exports are only a little over a third of the size of Korea's. However, at the same time India's need for export revenues is increasing.

Due to the adverse international political situation it is becoming increasingly difficult for India to obtain soft loans from multi lateral agencies. In 1983, 92% of total medium and long term (non - IMF) debt and 71% of the total increases in foreign debt were from public sources, yet in 1984 only 50% of the total increase in foreign loans were from public sources. The entry of China into the World Bank and the increasing needs of Eastern Europe had reduced India's privileged access to concessional external finance. Thus India has to borrow more and more from commercial sources which has resulted in higher interest and repayment burdens. India's outstanding foreign debt in 1979 was US $16 billion. In 1985 it went up to $ 25 billion and to about $42 billion in 1989. The ratio of debt service to GNP was 9.9% in 1979 and had reached 12.5% in 1989 and 16.6% in 1989. The amount of foreign debt was US$ 1.47 billion in 1980 and US $3.39 billion in 1985. The corresponding amounts of India's balance of payments deficit were US $1.7 billion on 1980 and US $3.45 billion in 1985.

Thus India's current problem in the balance of payments is mainly due to an increasing burden of debt services accompanied by increasing imports along with near stagnant exports.

Stagnation of India's export is a long term affair. The traditional items (Jute, Tea, Cotton and Textiles) are continuously losing their shares in the world market as other countries are developing better products at a lower price. At the same time as expected non traditional exports (i.e. manufacturing items) are gaining importance. However between 1960 and 1970, total imports of manufacturing of the industrialised world from developing countries rose by 260%; India only had expanded its exports to the industrialised world by 22% during the same period.

## Table 1.28
### Comparative export performances
### (annual % increase)

|         | 1980 | 1981 | 1982 | 1983 | 1984 | 1985 | 1986 |
|---------|------|------|------|------|------|------|------|
| India   | -0.5 | 3.5  | 4.9  | 2.9  | 2.9  | 2.5  | 4.3  |
| Korea   | 9.7  | 17.3 | 6.2  | 13.8 | 7.9  | 4.5  | 6.3  |
| Taiwan  | 9.3  | 11.8 | -3.2 | 13.4 | 10.8 | 2.0  | 6.6  |
| Malaysia| 1.8  | 6.0  | 6.3  | 13.9 | 11.7 | 2.0  | 4.8  |

Source: IMF.

As we can see from the above table, India's comparative performance during the 1980s, the most formidable period of growth for the Asian countries, was not impressive.

A variety of explorations are there behind these poor performances. The traditional view of the trade theorists (Bhagwati and Desai, 1965) was in terms of 'export pessimism' on the part of the government.

As a result exchange rate was not used to promote export. However, that explanation is not valid. 'Inward looking' development policies were pursued by a number of countries (like China, Japan, Korea), and these are some of the best examples of successful trading countries. The fact that devaluation can help export is not valid either. We can see from the table on exchange rates that both the effective exchange rate and the market exchange rate have undergone devaluation continuously, particularly since 1985, due to changes in tax subsidy rates.

However, we have not seen any improvements in India's export performance. Devaluation can theoretically reduce the prices of India's exports abroad so as to make them competitive. Nambiar and Mehta (1988) have shown (see Table 1.30), using relative price indices (ratio of foreign price US $ to domestic price in US $) of Indian industries, that except for Jute, Tea, Non ferrous metal items, electric motors, electric cable and some small manufacturing items, India export items have lower prices compared to their international prices. However, there are two reasons we should consider seriously. A country cannot export unless it can produce enough. If a country does not produce enough exportable surplus, there will not be an incentive for it to export. Because of low growth and a tax-subsidy system which works against exports, it is less profitable for the domestic firms to export than to sell in the home market (see Sau, 1988 and Table 1.31).

## Table 1.29
## Exchange rates and balance of payments

| year | exchange (1) (Rs/US $) | effective (2) exchange rate (E) | balance of (1) payments (mill US $) |
|---|---|---|---|
| 1970 | 7.5 | 1.24 | -411 |
| 1971 | 7.50 | 1.34 | -653 |
| 1972 | 7.59 | 1.41 | -167 |
| 1973 | 7.74 | 1.28 | -546 |
| 1974 | 8.10 | 1.24 | 1207 |
| 1975 | 8.37 | 1.20 | -148 |
| 1976 | 8.96 | 1.22 | 1579 |
| 1977 | 8.74 | 1.21 | 2119 |
| 1978 | 8.19 | 1.22 | 668 |
| 1979 | 8.12 | 1.21 | 50 |
| 1980 | 7.86 | 1.21 | -1785 |
| 1981 | 7.86 | 1.21 | -2698 |
| 1982 | 9.45 | 1.22 | -2524 |
| 1983 | 10.09 | 1.22 | -1930 |
| 1984 | 11.36 | 1.20 | -2343 |
| 1985 | 12.37 | 1.16 | -4177 |
| 1986 | 12.61 | 1.16 | -4597 |
| 1987 | 12.96 | 1.09 | -5192 |
| 1988 | 13.92 | 1.03 | -7148 |
| 1989 | 16.23 | -- | -- |
| 1990 | 17.50 | -- | -- |

Source: for (1) IMF.
(2) estimated from IMF, RBI, Ministry of Commerce, India.

Notes:
(a) First Plan: 51-56; Second Plan: 56-61; Third Plan: 61-65; Fourth Plan: 69-73; Fifth Plan: 74-78; Sixth Plan :80-85; Seventh Plan: 85-90.
(b) $E = EM/EX$. where $(R(1 + Sj)IWJ/IIj) = EM (or EX)$
EM = Effective exchange rate for imports; $IWj$ - World Inflation rate for $j$th export/or import.
EX = Effective exchange rate for export.
R = Nominal exchange rate (Rs/US $); $IIj$ - Indian inflation rate for $j$th export/or imports.
Sj = Net subsidy rate on the $j$th category of imports of exports.

## Table 1.30
### Relative price indices * of exports

| commodity | 1965 | 1975 | 1980 |
|---|---|---|---|
| Sugar | 103.72 | 288.75 | 168.87 |
| Tea/Coffee | 80.32 | 76.79 | 134.60 |
| Cotton Textile | 84.11 | 129.01 | 238.40 |
| Jute Textile | 62.44 | 69.54 | NA |
| Cement | 64.24 | 117.73 | 165.02 |
| Iron & Steel | 79.09 | 143.28 | 76.46 |
| Non Ferr.Metal | 66.89 | 80.70 | 100.38 |
| Metal Products | 121.88 | 168.93 | NA |
| Electric Motors | 109.76 | 95.78 | 201.75 |
| Electronics | 95.51 | 180.90 | NA |
| Elect. Appliances | 91.58 | 113.26 | NA |
| Elect. Wares, Cable | 56.70 | 95.61 | NA |
| Scientific Instruments | 135.77 | 215.74 | NA |
| Misc. Manufacturing | 77.78 | 60.02 | NA |

Source: Nambiar and Mehta (1988).
* World Price/Indian Price.

## Table 1.31
### Domestic resource cost, effective rate of protection and the rate of profit, 1980-81

| product group | domestic resource cost (Rs) | effective rate of protection % | | gross profit on export sales as % of export sales | | gross profit on domestic sales as % of domestic sales |
|---|---|---|---|---|---|---|
| | | export sales | domestic sales | without incentive | with incentive | |
| 1. Cables | 5.1 | 3.1 | -11.5 | 4.3 | 22.0 | 19.8 |
| 2. Auto Ancillaries | 5.5 | -22.0 | -15.6 | 4.2 | 17.0 | 21.6 |
| 3. Switchgear | 5.8 | -46.5 | 10.5 | 42.9 | 48.2 | 13.0 |
| 4. Steel Tubes | 5.9 | -18.9 | -20.2 | 40.8 | -23.5 | 13.1 |
| 5. Machine Tools | 6.2 | -3.0 | 8.5 | -30.8 | -11.8 | 23.3 |
| 6. Commercial Vehicles | 7.1 | 28.2 | 8.3 | 3.8 | 24.1 | 1.4 |
| 7. Ceramics | 7.6 | 32.3 | 35.4 | -34.1 | -20.9 | 29.0 |
| 8. Handtools | 7.9 | -18.0 | 53.5 | -8.5 | 3.3 | 21.4 |
| 9. Textiles | 10.2 | -17.9 | 65.4 | -18.0 | -6.4 | 9.2 |
| 10. Sheet Glass | 10.3 | 9.2 | -96.8 | -24.5 | -6.9 | 9.2 |
| 11. Wire Ropes | 10.4 | -68.6 | 103.1 | -14.9 | -1.2 | 14.1 |
| 12. Ferro. Alloys | 10.8 | -49.3 | 480.9 | 11.1 | 11.1 | 18.8 |
| 13. Textile Machinery | 11.1 | -11.9 | 101.4 | 1.0 | 16.1 | 17.0 |
| 14. Dyes | 11.9 | -68.5 | 469.2 | -57.3 | -31.2 | 13.8 |
| 15. Casting and Forging | 15.9 | -183.0 | 324.3 | -35.1 | -18.8 | 23.0 |

Source: Sau (1988)

Without any export incentives, only switchgear is profitable in the export market. However, although export incentive can make a lot of difference, it is not enough.

### Table 1.32
### Comparative growth rates of Asian countries (real GNP)

| year | 1981 | 1982 | 1983 | 1984 | 1985 | 1986 | 1987 | 1988 | 1989 |
|---|---|---|---|---|---|---|---|---|---|
| India | 6.0 | 3.7 | 7.8 | 3.8 | 6.3 | 4.7 | 1.7 | 6.2 | 4.7 |
| China | 5.4 | 8.7 | 10.1 | 13.5 | 12.3 | 9.3 | 9.4 | 7.8 | 7.6 |
| Korea | 7.4 | 5.7 | 10.9 | 8.6 | 5.4 | 11.9 | 10.9 | 7.8 | 5.2 |
| Taiwan | 6.1 | 2.8 | 7.7 | 9.6 | 4.3 | 10.6 | 11.3 | 5.1 | 6.5 |
| Singapore | 9.9 | 6.3 | 7.9 | 8.2 | -1.8 | 1.9 | 8.6 | 6.9 | 5.3 |
| Malaysia | 6.9 | 5.9 | 6.3 | 7.8 | -1.0 | 1.2 | 3.1 | 5.1 | 5.1 |

Source: IMF.
* In constant 1970 prices and exchange rate

The comparative performances of different Asian countries can explain the poor performance of Indian exports. As we can see from the above, growth rate of the real GDP of India is quite low for most of these years compared to other Asian countries which are successful in exports. In particular, if we compare India and China the difference is quite significant. That can explain the dismal performance of India's exports, compared to that of China. Comparison with China is meaningful because China has followed the so-called 'inward looking - development policy' (i.e industrialization under trade protection) but it is successful in exports.

### Table 1.33
### Comparative export* performances:
### India and China (annual % charge)

| year | 1981 | 1982 | 1983 | 1984 | 1985 | 1986 | 1987 | 1988 | 1989 |
|---|---|---|---|---|---|---|---|---|---|
| India | 3.5 | 4.9 | 2.9 | 2.8 | -5.8 | 8.1 | 10.5 | 7.6 | 8.1 |
| China | 32.5 | 13.3 | 4.7 | 25.4 | 29.1 | 24.1 | 29.7 | 13.0 | 14.8 |

Source: IMF.
* Real Export in Constant 1980 prices.

If we compare growth performances, we can see the reason. Because China was growing at a much faster rate, it had generated exportable surpluses, it was no longer profitable to sell at home, so it had to look for markets abroad. For India, because of slower growth, exportable surpluses were not generated and there was no incentive for India to sell abroad.

In view of the above discussion, we are in a realistic position to analyse the exchange rate mechanism. After the Smithsonian agreement in 1971, rupee was pegged to pound for intervention in the exchange rate until 1975. After 1975, rupee was related to a basket of currency with Pound as the dominant currency. In that basket a margin of variation of 2 to 5 percent was allowed, which was raised to 9 per cent in 1979. The rate of changes of nominal and real effective exchange rates and the real exports are given below, which will show that we cannot see any significant relationship between the exchange rate (nominal or effective) to the growth rates of exports.

### Table 1.34
### Nominal exchange rate, real exchange rate and real export growth
### (annual % charge)

| year | nominal exchange rate | real effective rate (1980=1) | real export |
|---|---|---|---|
| 1981 | -10.1 | 1.2 | 3.5 |
| 1982 | -9.2 | 0.0 | 4.9 |
| 1983 | -6.8 | 3.7 | 2.9 |
| 1984 | -12.5 | -3.3 | 2.8 |
| 1985 | -8.9 | -5.0 | -5.8 |
| 1986 | -2.0 | -10.7 | 8.1 |
| 1987 | -2.7 | -5.5 | 10.5 |
| 1988 | -3.2 | -5.6 | 7.6 |
| 1989 | -5.5 | -5.6 | 8.1 |
| Period Av | -6.7 | -3.4 | 4.7 |

The exchange rate was used and probably will be used to control inflows and outflows of monetary resources where it will be most effective. Little and Joshi (1987) had put forward the argument that during 1974-78 the real effective exchange rate was declined by 23 per cent and the real export went up by 11 per cent. That is a spurious relationship because we know that during that period India had suddenly increased its exports to the Middle East after the first 'oil-crisis' of 1974. During the following period of 1979-83, India's exports to the Middle East had stagnated due to the reductions of the purchasing powers of the Middle East Countries as oil prices could not grow as fast as it was expected and the Middle East economy went through re-adjustments of their expenditures.

## Table 1.35
## foreign debt - India
## (millions of current US dollars)

|  | 1981 | 1982 | 1983 | 1984 | 1985 | 1986 |
|---|---|---|---|---|---|---|
| | | | foreign debt indicators | | | |
| total foreign debt | 20.749 | 24.921 | 28.371 | 30.986 | 35.405 | 39.281 |
| of which medium & long term | 19.545 | 23.094 | 26.798 | 29.243 | 33.889 | 36.967 |
| short term | 1.204 | 1.327 | 1.573 | 1.743 | 1.516 | 2.314 |
| total amortization | 1.648 | 2.090 | 2.803 | 2.662 | 3.670 | 3.607 |
| of which medium & long term | 722 | 886 | 976 | 1,089 | 1.927 | 2.091 |
| short term | 926 | 1.204 | 1.827 | 1.573 | 1.743 | 1.516 |
| total interest payments | 617 | 853 | 923 | 1.102 | 1.599 | 1.778 |
| of which medium & long term | 411 | 606 | 767 | 908 | 1.468 | 1.614 |
| short term | 207 | 247 | 156 | 194 | 131 | 164 |
| total debt service | 2.265 | 2.943 | 3.726 | 3.764 | 5.184 | 5.330 |
| of which medium & long term | 1.133 | 1.492 | 1.743 | 1.997 | 3.310 | 3.650 |
| short term | 1.133 | 1.451 | 1.983 | 1.767 | 1.874 | 1.680 |
| | | | underlying factors | | | |
| current account | -2.699 | -2.523 | -1.932 | -2.343 | -4.214 | -4.072 |
| foreign investment | 0 | 0 | 0 | 0 | 0 | 173 |
| change in reserves | -2.251 | -378 | 622 | 905 | 578 | -24 |
| net borrowing requirement | 1.597 | 4.172 | 3.450 | 2.615 | 4.420 | 3.875 |
| amortization (m & l term debt) | 722 | 886 | 976 | 1.089 | 1.927 | 2.091 |
| gross borrowing requirement | 2.319 | 5.058 | 4.426 | 3.704 | 6.347 | 5.966 |

## Table 1.35 - continued
## foreign debt - India
## (millions of current US dollars)

|  | 1987 | 1988 | 1989 | 1990 | 1991 | 1992 |
|---|---|---|---|---|---|---|
| | | | foreign debt indicators | | | |
| total foreign debt | 42.092 | 45.744 | 49.973 | 54.096 | 57.972 | 62.133 |
| of which medium & long term | 39.509 | 42.888 | 46.811 | 50.633 | 54.240 | 58.132 |
| short term | 2.542 | 2.826 | 3.152 | 3.453 | 3.741 | 4.032 |
| total amortization | 5.076 | 5.979 | 6.564 | 6.705 | 7.244 | 7.763 |
| of which medium & long term | 2.763 | 3.437 | 3.737 | 3.554 | 3.791 | 4.022 |
| short term | 2.314 | 2.542 | 2.826 | 3.152 | 3.453 | 3.741 |
| total interest payments | 1.672 | 1.819 | 1.872 | 2.052 | 2.052 | 2.329 |
| of which medium & long term | 1.483 | 1.627 | 1.634 | 1.779 | 2.024 | 2.271 |
| short term | 189 | 192 | 238 | 272 | 305 | 333 |
| total debt service | 6.677 | 7.724 | 8.371 | 8.716 | 9.573 | 10.367 |
| of which medium & long term | 4.175 | 4.990 | 5.307 | 5.292 | 5.815 | 6.293 |
| short term | 2.503 | 2.734 | 3.064 | 3.424 | 3.758 | 4.074 |
| | | | underlying factors | | | |
| current account | -3.733 | -3.873 | -4.148 | -4.324 | -4.431 | -4.519 |
| foreign investment | 275 | 382 | 525 | 613 | 760 | 908 |
| change in reserves | -647 | 161 | 605 | 413 | 205 | 550 |
| net borrowing requirement | 2.811 | 3.653 | 4.228 | 4.123 | 3.876 | 4.161 |
| amortization (m & l term debt) | 2.763 | 3.437 | 3.737 | 3.554 | 3.791 | 4.022 |
| gross borrowing requirement | 5.574 | 7.090 | 7.966 | 7.677 | 7.677 | 8.182 |

## Table 1.36
## medium and long term debt - India
## (millions of current US dollars)

|  | 1981 | 1982 | 1983 | 1984 | 1985 | 1986 |
|---|---|---|---|---|---|---|
| | \multicolumn{6}{c}{medium and long term debt outstanding} | | | | | |
| public guarant - official | 17.254 | 18.393 | 19.460 | 19.850 | 23.201 | 25.663 |
| private | 729 | 1.118 | 1.692 | 2.445 | 3.449 | 3.956 |
| private non guarant | 873 | 1.239 | 1.767 | 2.611 | 3.093 | 3.661 |
| liability to IMF | 689 | 2.343 | 3.879 | 4.337 | 4.147 | 3.686 |
| | \multicolumn{6}{c}{interest payments} | | | | | |
| public guarant - official | 345 | 359 | 418 | 436 | 511 | 537 |
| private | 29 | 111 | 149 | 244 | 290 | 368 |
| private non guarant | 37 | 136 | 200 | 228 | 265 | 351 |
| liability to IMF | 0 | 0 | 0 | 0 | 402 | 358 |
| | \multicolumn{6}{c}{amortizations} | | | | | |
| public guarant - official | 579 | 603 | 600 | 549 | 630 | 707 |
| private | 58 | 64 | 115 | 235 | 454 | 428 |
| private non guarant | 85 | 219 | 261 | 305 | 653 | 495 |
| liability to IMF | 0 | 0 | 0 | 0 | 190 | 461 |

1. public guarant - official: publically guaranteed debt from official sources.

2. public guarant - private: publically guaranteed debt from private sources.

3. private non guarant: private non guaranteed debt from all sources.

## Table 1.36 - continued
## medium and long term debt - India
## (millions of current US dollars)

|  | 1987 | 1988 | 1989 | 1990 | 1991 | 1992 |
|---|---|---|---|---|---|---|
| | \multicolumn{6}{c}{medium and long term debt outstanding} | | | | | |
| public guarant - official | 28.351 | 31.626 | 34.706 | 37.463 | 39.972 | 42.425 |
| private | 3.884 | 3.984 | 4.965 | 6.012 | 7.120 | 8.318 |
| private non guarant | 4.328 | 5.186 | 5.777 | 6.331 | 6.858 | 7.389 |
| liability to IMF | 2.946 | 2.092 | 1.363 | 827 | 291 | 0 |
| | \multicolumn{6}{c}{interest payments} | | | | | |
| public guarant - official | 527 | 616 | 671 | 665 | 749 | 829 |
| private | 334 | 387 | 374 | 443 | 561 | 669 |
| private non guarant | 336 | 422 | 456 | 591 | 686 | 773 |
| liability to IMF | 286 | 203 | 132 | 80 | 28 | 0 |
| | \multicolumn{6}{c}{amortizations} | | | | | |
| public guarant - official | 832 | 1.051 | 1.295 | 1.340 | 1.475 | 1.568 |
| private | 609 | 852 | 901 | 817 | 852 | 1.169 |
| private non guarant | 580 | 680 | 812 | 860 | 928 | 994 |
| liability to IMF | 741 | 854 | 729 | 536 | 536 | 291 |

1. public guarant - official: publically guaranteed debt from official sources.

2. public guarant - private: publically guaranteed debt from private sources.

3. private non guarant: private non guaranteed debt from all sources.

## New economic policies

India is going through a difficult period mainly due to adverse international developments. The 'Gulf War' over Kuwait in 1990 has destroyed a major source of India's foreign exchange earnings. First the market for India's exports to Iraq and Kuwait was eliminated and at the same time, Indian workers employed in those two countries have lost their jobs and India has lost their remittances. At the same time, desolvation of the Soviet Union brought a crisis for India. The former Soviet Union was the most important market for Indian exports and at the same time India used to import from the Soviet Union quite heavily due to the fact that the payment could be in terms of rupee. Erosion of the Soviet Union thus has created a large gap in the Indian economy which will take several years to fill up.

As a result of these extraordinary circumstances, India has recently decided to intensify the process that was started in 1985 i.e. to reform the economy particularly on the trade policy and on the industrial policy.

The so-called 'New Economic Policy' is centred around three main issues: Reform of Trade Policy, Reform of the Industrial Policy towards the private sector and the fiscal policy particularly that related to the subsidy structure. On the trade policy, it was a long standing issue among the trade theorists that the Government had not promoted exports because of the import substitution policies. The remedy suggested was to remove the protection on the industrial sector and open the economy for imports and at the same time use devaluation as an instrument to promote export rather than the existing export promotion measures (for details see Basu and Bala-Subramaniym, 1991). The Indian rupee was devalued in 1991 for that purpose by about 40 per cent. However, from the discussion on the exchange rate we have seen, the devaluation will have little impact on Indian exports revenues, unless India makes significant effort to create the marketing system for India's exports. Removals of existing export promotion measures on the other hand will make export unprofitable for domestic firms. At the same time, India's balance of payments position is grave, so India's ability to import is questionable. Removal of import restrictions is not a suitable option given their condition and it is not clear what benefit the economy may derive. At the same time, complete removal of import restriction will also create a massive unemployment because the domestic firms are ill equipped to compete. Thus complete removal of import restrictions are not on the agenda, however, tariff rates are reduced and import procedures are simplified to make way for further import liberalization.

The new 'Industrial Policy' has deregulated a large part of the industrial sector; thus private sectors will have access to most parts of the manufacturing sector and licensing is no longer needed for most of the manufacturing activities. This measure is welcomed by both the private sector and the economists as this will free the domestic private sector from excessive control. Previously the licensing system which was designed in the '1956 Industrial Policy' to regulate the economy in a socially desirable manner was much abused. It was used to promote monopoly power among some of the business classes favoured by the government. It was also used to redirect industries to particular areas favoured by the politicians irrespective of the suitability of area for that particular industry or of the need of the economy. Subsidy systems whose purposes should be to allocate resources efficiently by driving prices towards the efficient prices were also abused in a similar way to favour particular business groups and particular regions. Reforms are needed in these two areas of industrial policies and are welcomed. However, the 'New Economic Policy' so far shows signs of the old system i.e. political discretions. Petrochemicals and car manufacturing are preserved in the licensed sector in order to protect some favoured business group. Subsidies on agriculture were reduced which will turn the intersectional terms of trade between agriculture and Industry against agriculture thereby undermining future agricultural growth. Removal of subsidies for urban population will increase the cost of living for industrial workers which will create more wage demands and inflation will follow. Removal of subsidies on education will make education inaccessible for the majority of the people. However, the subsidy on transport (i.e. freight rate equalization subsidies) was not touched yet. The main object of this subsidy is to equalise the cost of some important strategic and industrial raw materials (e.g. iron, steel, coal, metals etc) across the country. The effect of this subsidy so far is to create regional imbalance in favour of Western regions. However, because of political reasons this subsidy has not been removed although it can save a lot of unnecessary expenses.

At the same time interest rates on bank advances are very high (about 21 per cent in 1991), given that very few private industries will be in a position to expand unless the cost of borrowing can be reduced.

India has recently accepted loans from the IMF to overcome balance of payment difficulties. The so called 'New Economic Policy' is not very different from the standard IMF World bank 'structural adjustment programme' which IMF has used in Africa extensively with variable results. In view of that an examination of the IMF-World Bank policies is necessary.

## Table 1.37
## Nominal and real effective exchange rates; 1980 = 1

|  | 1981 | 1982 | 1983 | 1984 | 1985 | 1986 | 1987 | 1988 |
|---|---|---|---|---|---|---|---|---|
| Nominal Effective Exchange Rate | .97 | .96 | .92 | .85 | .79 | .65 | .59 | .51 |
| % Charges | -2.3 | -1.6 | -4.1 | -7.4 | -6.9 | -17.12 | -10.5 | -12.7 |
| Real Effective Exchange Rate | 1.01 | 1.01 | 1.05 | 1.01 | .96 | .86 | .81 | .76 |
| % Charges | 1.2 | 0.0 | 3.7 | -3.3 | -5.0 | -10.7 | -5.5 | -5.6 |

Source: IMF.

### IMF conditionalities and their effects

It is well known that countries under IMF surveillance (such as India) need to adopt certain economic policies (the so called IMF conditions) the most important of which are the exchange rate and fiscal measures designed to put their economies back on course. From past experience, the general consensus is that IMF policies bring long-term disaster and are highly inefficient even with respect to short-term stabilization. A number of recent studies have tried to point out the fallacies of their approach and the intellectual responses of the IMF are quite formidable (Hassain and Thirwall, 1984; Branson, 1983; Killick, 1984; Nashahibi, 1980 and Goldstein, 1986).

The 'Structural Adjustment Programme' of the World Bank which is designed to transform a public-controlled economy to a market based economy has implemented the traditional IMF measures in a number of African and Latin American countries but has failed to achieve the desired results (for the analysis of the IMF conditionalities on Africa see Basu, 1987). The IMF can be criticised for taking insufficient account of structural rigidities, political and institutional constraints and non-financial objectives (like food security, distribution of income, basic desires of the people regarding the goals and developments) in its country level policy packages (Killick, 1984). Particularly controversial is the efficiency of such IMF-World Bank measures such as:-

(a) Massive devaluations and/or floating exchange rate.
(b) Increased nominal interest rate.
(c) General liberalization of import controls.
(d) Generalized expansion of primary commodity exports.
(e) Sale of large scale public enterprise to the private sector.

The forced adjustment imposed by short-term balance of payments arithmetic, it was argued, not only makes the investment required for recovery implausible, but also damages the limited and painfully accumulated existing capital stock, worse since it results in unnecessary current output losses and under-utilization of essentially non-tradeable sectors.

The IMF conditionality has concentrated on two major macro policy aspects: adequate exchange rate management and demand discipline. The latter is to be achieved through fiscal restraint and limited expansion of net domestic credit. The theory is that wage-price flexibility leads to full employment equilibrium and that private savings and investment are not affected by budgetary cuts. As public sector deficit will imply deficit in the current account of the balance of payments, practical effects of any reduction in the public sector deficit will be improvements in the current account of the balance of payments. Inflation is to be controlled through monetary policy so that the political temptation of exchange rate overvaluation does not arise.

However, IMF conditionalities are biased towards recession because they overlook wage/price rigidity and the fact that wages in a developing country, in most cases, are subsistence wages. A complicating factor is that some required adjustment policies, including exchange rate devaluation, indirect tax increases and reduction in subsidies imply a temporary acceleration of inflation. Wage/price stickiness combined with contradictory aggregate demand policies can lead to dismal stagflation.

**Appropriate exchange rate**

What should be the appropriate level of devaluation under such structural constraints? The size and nature of the external shocks that an open economy faces may be important determinants of the optimal degree of exchange rate flexibility. For developing countries where foreign exchange markets are not well developed, the monetary authorities set and announce the exchange rate at which transactions are to take place and at which they will buy and sell foreign exchange from and to the financial intermediaries. The monetary authorities directly determine the value of the domestic currency in relation to the interest on currency by adopting a price-setting rule. With an adjustable peg the exchange rate of the domestic currency is kept constant against a single foreign currency or average of foreign currencies, which is the Indian system. In India the rupee was pegged to the British pound and then to set currencies with variable weights. An alternative is to include in the price setting rule more continuous reference to some set of variables or indicators, an exchange rate regime using a form of crawling peg or gliding parity. Williamson (1982) has recommended an overall exchange rate policy that is dedicated to preserving the constancy of the real exchange rate except when there is a perceived need to change the real exchange to promote external payment adjustments. He argues that the most efficient way to preserve a constant real exchange rate is to use a crawling peg based on a relative inflation rate indication. An inflation rate differential also forms part of the policy rule for exchange rate management articulated by Cline (1978). The practicability of this policy can be questioned because of the lack of timely price data. The solution can be that the current inflation rate can be estimated from the known price data using an auto-regressive technique.

However, this crawling peg method may be insufficient to maintain external balance. Changes in economic conditions or circumstances that a developing country confronts, such as terms of trade shock may call for a change in exchange rate and other policies to affect an alteration in the real exchange rate for external balance adjustment.

The formal objective of the IMF supported adjustment programme is to bring about a viable balance of payments in the medium term. The formulation of exchange rate policies in such a programme has taken into account the overall stance of domestic and foreign policies as well as prospective internal and external conditions over the medium term. Assessment of the degree of responsiveness of the elements of the balance of payments to exchange rate changes (elasticity analysis) is integral to the formulation of exchange rate policies; often the use of elasticities is implicit. The size and speed of the domestic supply response depend on the extent to which it results from (1) putting to use previously idle resources; (2) increased productivity - through more intensive use of resources; (3) movement of resources from the non-tradeable to the tradeable sector; and (4) movement of resources within the tradeable goods sector.

Exchange rate changes in nominal terms can spark off domestic cost inflation thereby presenting a real devaluation, but this is not inevitable. Much depends on the content of the policy packages of which exchange rate depreciations are part. One immediate impact of devaluation will be to raise government receipts by expanding the local currency value of the bases for import and export taxes. This positive impact of devaluation on government resources will be diluted to the extent that trade taxes are specific rather than ad-valorem and to the extent that there exists exemption from import duties. Another immediate impact of devaluation will be to raise the local currency value of foreign capital inflows. Devaluation also means a corresponding increase in the local currency value of the import component of public expenditure. The item of public expenditure which is all in foreign exchange is debt service on foreign borrowing. Such outlay has been growing rapidly and can be quite large particularly if account is taken not only of central government obligation but also of debts guaranteed by the government. Thus devaluation will trigger a number of partly off-setting repercussions and the net outcome will be uncertain.

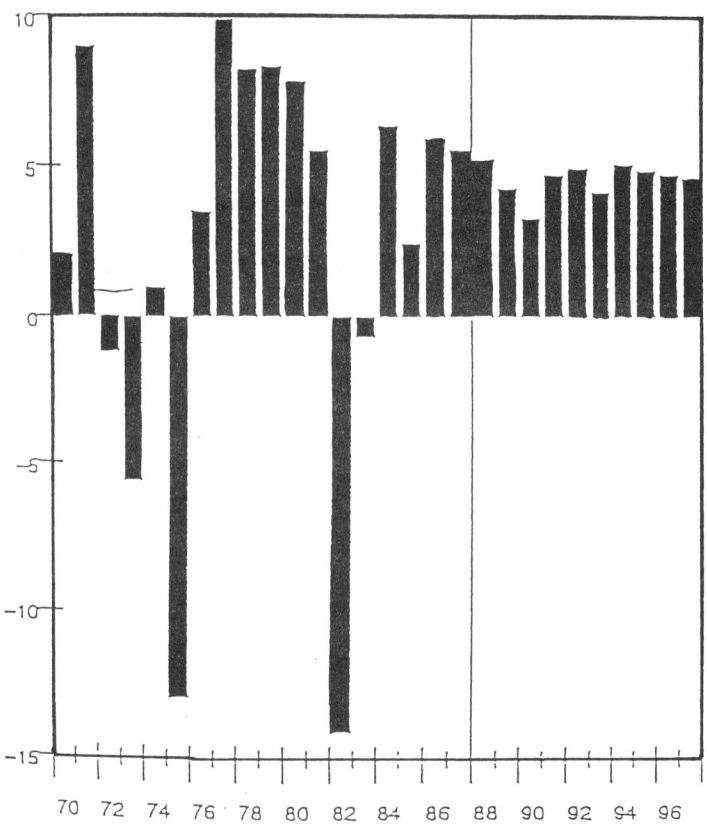

**Figure 1.11 Gross Domestic Product – Chile (% change from a year ago)**

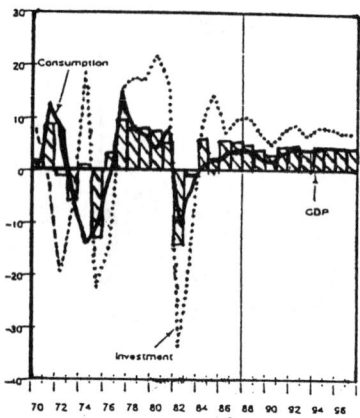

**Figure 1.12  GDP and Domestic Demand – Chile (% change from a year ago)**

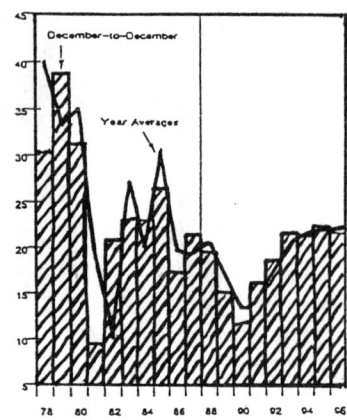

**Figure 1.13  Annual CPI Inflation – Chile**

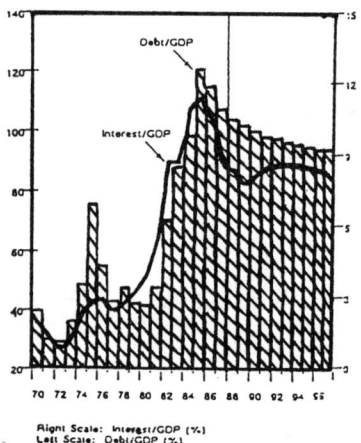

**Figure 1.14  Foreign Debt as % of GDP – Chile**

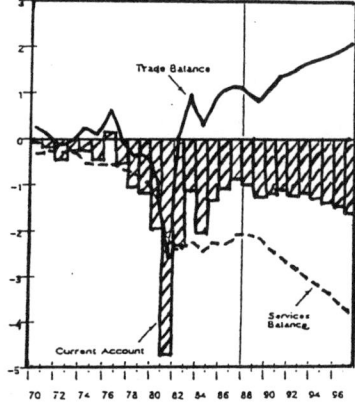

**Figure 1.15  Current Account Balance – Chile (billions of U.S. dollars)**

## Evaluations of IMF - World Bank Programme

It is difficult to evaluate export on the outcome of the structural adjustment programme because the circumstances for the country in question can change for the better or for the worse due to some external reasons. Recently Egypt and Nigeria have accepted the IMF - World Bank programme in 1987-88. However, in the case of Egypt, due to political consideration, its foreign debt was written off by the USA and the subsequent improvements in the export revenues of oil have reduced Egypt's financial crisis. Similarly Nigeria has experienced more than 100 per cent increase in her oil revenue in 1991 due to the Gulf War but Nigeria's balance of payments problems are far from over. In neither case can we say IMF - World Bank Policies have created a favourable situation. Similarly although India had achieved her 'Green Revolutions' in 1966-67 when the economy was under the IMF supervision, the IMF policies had nothing to contribute towards the 'Green Revolution'. However, it is possible to evaluate the long term effects of the IMF - World Bank programme if we consider a country which has followed these policies consistently over a prolonged period of time. One such country is Chile, which had introduced the economic programme after the downfall of Allende Government in 1973 which has every characteristic of the so-called 'Structural Adjustment Programme'. If we consider the period between 1972 and 1987 (the sudden increases in the price of copper in 1987, Chile's major export earner can distort the comparison if we consider any later years), we can see the effect of the IMF programme on Chile's economy. From the graph we can see quite easily the IMF programme could not have stabilised the economy; the cycles in GDP growth rate, investment rate and domestic consumptions are quite prominent. Although the rate of growth of the GDP is about 6 per cent in 1987 compared to about 1 per cent in 1973-74, the rate of investment in 1987 was about 9 per cent compared to about 20 per cent in 1973-74. The inflation rate in 1987 was about 23 per cent, in 1980 it was about 38 per cent. The real exchange rate declined sharply from 1972 until 1980, since then it has improved a little. However, the balance of payment situation in 1987 was much worse than in 1973-74. As a result, when in 1972 the ratio of debt to GDP was about 20 per cent, in 1987 it became about 105 per cent, thus making Chile insolvent. Thus although the IMF programme had increased the rate of growth of the GDP, the cost to the country in terms of debt was enormous. The reduction in the real exchange rate has not improved the balance of payments. The Chilean experience shows the IMF programme was implemented against a cost to the people, therefore its pure economic achievement are of dubious values.

Historical experience from Germany, Hungary and Austria shows (Franco, 1990) that a stabilization programme during 1922-24 to combat hyper-inflation and foreign debt problem was in terms of increased resource mobilization rather than through massive reductions in public expenditures as IMF - World Bank suggests. In the classic German case, the levels of expenditure before and after the stabilization were very similar. Similar reforms were introduced by the League of Nations in Austria and Hungary in 1922-24, namely there were predominant changes in the composition of expenditure (i.e. increased emphasis on public investment rather than government consumptions) with little effect on the level of expenditure. Tax resources in all cases were increased due to price stability forced by the Governments. This means budget deficits were to an overhelming extent products of inflation and the deficits were eliminated mostly by the effect of price stability on tax revenues (i.e. Oliverira-Tanzi effect (1967, 1987); the fact that tax revenues were negatively affected by inflation). It suggests that fiscal balance was not a sufficient condition for stabilization when other fundamental causes of inflation were still in full work.

*Concluding comments*

Although the so-called 'New Economic Policy' was apparently designed by the new finance minister of India in 1991, we can see quite easily it is nothing but the standard IMF - World Bank induced 'Structural Adjustment Programme', whose main goal is to transform the economy from a publicly controlled to a market-driven system. Historical experience shows that the probability of success is low and the danger of India falling into a debt-trap is quite significant. Although the deregulation of the private sector will stimulate the economy, the inability to finance imports will be a serious obstacle for growth. Monetary-fiscal and financial policies should be co-ordinated in order to achieve a long term sustainable growth rather than a short term stability. The purpose of the research is to evaluate and narrate such co-ordinated policies.

# 2 Method of optimal control

## Introduction

The purpose of this chapter is to explain and elaborate the fundamental principles of 'control' methods. Although we owe our debt to the Soviet mathematician, Pontryagin *et al.* (1962), for the analytical developments of the optimal control techniques, we have seen major advances in recent years in the direction of estimation and control of econometric models. Econometric models pose different sets of problems than one can encounter in an algebraic model. The usefulness of 'optimal control' methods depends on their usefulness in controlling practical models and to generate realistic solutions. In reality, expectation structures can play a very important role in shaping the directions and attainabilities of policy prescriptions. 'Filtering' approach and 'Stochastic' control systems are designed to solve these problems (Tse and Athans, 1972; Basu and Lazardis, 1986).

## Deterministic control

The optimal control technique can deal with general constraints on the control variables. In the algebraic formulation a general purpose control problem can be described as follows (see Pontryagin, 1962).

$$\text{Max } J_{\{u(t)\}} = \int_{t_0}^{t_1} I(x, u, t)dt + F(x_1, t_1)$$

$$\dot{x} = f(x, u, t)$$

$$x(t_0) = x_0$$

$$x(t_1) = x_1$$

$$\{u(t)\} \in U$$

When $I(x, u, t)$ is the objective function expressed in terms of state variable $x$, control variable $u$ and time $t$; $t_0$ is the starting point of the plan and $t_1$ is the terminal point; $x(t_0)$ is the state variable in the initial period, $x(t_1)$ is the planned target to be achieved. The system $f(x, u, t)$ describes the dynamics of the state variable and its relationship with the control variables and time. $F(x_1, t_1)$ is the terminal condition. In the algebraic solution we can assume $I(\ldots)$, $F(\ldots)$, and $f(\ldots)$ are continuously differentiate functions.

$\{u(t)\}$ is the control trajectory belonging to a constrained control set $U$. State variable can be of any real numbers

$$X(t) = (x_1(t), x_2(t), \ldots x_n(t))$$

$$t_0 < t < t_1$$

Thus $\{X(t)\} = \{X(t) \in E^n \mid t_0 < t < t_1\}$
when $E^n$ is the Euclidean $n$-space.

Similarly control variables can be of any $r$ real numbers subject to certain constraint on their possible values. Suppose there are $r$ control variables

$$U(t) = (u_1(t), u_2(t), \ldots u_r(t))'$$

$$\{u(t)\} = \{u(t) \in E^r \mid t_0 < t < t_1\}$$

$\{u(t)\}$ is a piecewise continuous vector valued function of time and the control vector $u(t)$ at all time must belong to a given non-empty subset of Euclidean $r$-space $\Omega$ so that

$$u(t) \in \Omega, \ t_0 < t < t_1,$$

where $\Omega$ is compact (closed and bounded), convex and time invariant. The control set $U$ is the set of the admissible control trajectories.

$$\{u(t)\} \subset U$$

Control variables can be of two types: 'open' loop and 'closed' loop. In 'open' loop control variables are specified and determined in advance and state trajectories are determined accordingly. In the 'closed' loop control optimal control trajectory is determined as a function of the current state variable and time, $\{u^*(x(t), t)\}$, so that the decisions may be revised in the light of new information embodied in the current state variables.

Although algebraic formulation as given above can be of immense use in theoretical economics, if we want to apply optimal control system in econometric models we need to work with linear systems which are amenable to computational requirements. The linear optimal control system can be described as follows.

$$\max_{\{u(t)\}} J = \frac{1}{2}\int_{t_0}^{t_1}(x'dx + u'Eu)dt + \frac{1}{2}x'_1 F x_1$$

$$\dot{x} = Ax + BU$$

$$x(t_0) = x_0$$

$$x(t_1) = x_1$$

when $D$ and $F$ are matrices of order $n$, $E$ is a matrix of order $r$ and $A$ and $B$ are given matrix of size $n \times n$ and $n \times r$

In this particular case we can form a function (Hamiltonian) which is to be minimized subject to the

$$H = \frac{1}{2}(x'Dx + u'Eu) + y(Ax + Bu)$$

where $y$ is the co-state variables. The optimality conditions are as follows

$$\frac{dH}{du} = u'E + yB = 0 \Rightarrow u^* = -E^{-1}B'y'$$

$$\dot{x} = \frac{dH}{dy} = Ax + Bu = Ax - BE^{-1}B'y'$$

$$\dot{y} = -\frac{dH}{dy} = x'D - yA$$

$$y(t_1) = x'_1 F$$

$$x(t_0) = x_0$$

If we assume a linear solution of the form

$$y = x'Q(t)$$

where $Q$ is $n \times n$ matrix with elements varying over time. We can derive a 'Ricatti' equation for $Q(t)$:

$$\dot{Q} - QBE^{-1}B'Q + QA + A'Q + D = 0$$

with $Q(t_1) = F$

Finally we can obtain $u^*(t) = -E^{-1}B'Q'(t) \times (t)$, which is the optimal closed loop control.

A number of authors have used the above method to derive algorithms to solve a linear econometric system with quadratic cost criteria* (Pindyck, 1973). However there is an alternative method which can be useful if we can incorporate uncertainty in a very simple way. Another advantage of our proposed method is that we can derive a closed form solution (as opposed to iterative solutions).

## Deterministic control using pseudo-inverse

The method proposed (Basu and Lazaridis, 1983) gives a closed form solution for a certain class of optimal control problem by means of a generalized pseudo-inverse matrix. Among the practical advantages are that for a multi-variable control problem it does not create any problem of dimensionality for a moderate size problem. Because of the use of pseudo-inverse it is possible to have more control variable than the state variable in the system and still we can obtain the (minimum norm) solution.

The basic theorem we are going to use is due to Penrose (1955, 1956) and Greville (1960) which is as follows:
The best approximate solution $U^*$ of a system of the form $AU = B$ is such that for all $U$ either

$$\| AU - B \| > \| AU^* - B \|$$

or

$$\| AU - B \| = \| AU^* - B \| \text{ and } \| U \| \geq \| U^* \|$$

Thus $U^*$ has least norm which minimizes the sum of squares $\| AU - B \|^2$. The best approximate solution is given by $U^* = A^+ B$ where $A^+$ is the pseudo inverse of $A$.

To illustrate our method let us proceed with a deterministic system

$$X(t+1) = AX(t) + BU(t) \quad t = 0 \ldots N \tag{1}$$

where $X \in E^n$, $U \in E^m$ $A \in E^{n \times n}$ and $B \in E^{n \times m}$ are coefficient matrices.

The system state at the terminal period is given by

$$X(N) = A^N X(0) + RV \tag{2}$$

---

\* The algorithm involves solutions of the 'Ricatti' equation and computation of stable and control variable accordingly.

where
$$V = \{U(0), U(1), \ldots U(N-1)\}$$
$$R = \{A^{N-1}B, \ldots, AB, B\} \text{ and } X(0) \text{ is the initial state.}$$

For any $N > n$, the controllability matrix is a submatrix of $R$ as defined above, which implies that rank $(R) = n$; if we assume the system is controllable (see appendix) since the initial and terminal conditions are fixed points in the $n$-dimensional Euclidean space, equation for terminal state can be reduced to

$$RV = b \tag{3}$$

where $b = X(N) - A^N X(0)$

suppose a quadratic performance criterion is

$$f = \sum_{j=1}^{N} (D_j U - S_j)' Q_j (D_j U - S_j) \tag{4}$$

where $Q_j = R'_j R_j$

[Assuming that $Q$ is positive definite and symmetric it can be easily decomposed using Cholesky's factorization method. If $Q$ is not symmetric initially it can be transformed to a symmetric matrix

$$Q^s = \tfrac{1}{2}(Q+Q)$$

so that the considered quadratic form remains unchanged.]

The system is represented here by

$$D_j X = S_j; \ldots j = 1 \ldots N$$

we can rewrite (4) as follows

$$f = \sum_{j=1}^{N} (D_j U - S_j)' R'_j R (D_j U - S_j)$$

$$= \begin{bmatrix} R_1(D_1 U - S_1) \\ R_2(D_2 U - S_2) \\ R_N(D_N U - S_N) \end{bmatrix}' \begin{bmatrix} R_1(D_1 U - S_1) \\ R_2(D_2 U - S_2) \\ R_N(D_N U - S_N) \end{bmatrix}$$

$$= \left\| \begin{bmatrix} R_1 D_1 \\ \cdot \\ \cdot \\ R_N D_N \end{bmatrix} U - \begin{bmatrix} R_1 S_1 \\ \cdot \\ \cdot \\ R_N S_N \end{bmatrix} \right\|^2$$

Thus the optimal control law is given by

$$U^* = \begin{bmatrix} R_1 D_1 \\ \cdot \\ \cdot \\ R_N D_N \end{bmatrix}^+ \cdot \begin{bmatrix} R_1 S_1 \\ \cdot \\ \cdot \\ R_N S_N \end{bmatrix} \qquad (5)$$

The optimal control involves minimum norm solution. This implies if we arrange the instruments of the system properly, the control rule can drive the system to the desired state with minimum efforts. Although one may argue that this can sometimes be achieved by rearranging the associated weight matrix of the control vector, in practice this involves an enormous amount of computational effort because the optimum paths of the state vector are very sensitive to the weight matrix of the control vector. By having a minimum norm solution we can avoid these inconveniences.

## Stochastic simulations

The simplest way we can add uncertainty into the system is to incorporate an additional stochastic variable i.e. additive error. The addition of the disturbance term does not change the system equation significantly but it would change the time path of state and control variables and the value of the cost function. Let us consider a stochastic system which is assumed to be controllable.

$$X(t) = AX(t-1) + BU(t) + C\varepsilon(t)$$

where $\varepsilon$ is the $n$-dimensional noise vector with as many non-zero elements as the number of stochastic relations in the model. It is usually assumed the noise is normally distributed Gaussian and

$$E(\varepsilon(t)) = 0, \quad E(\varepsilon(t), \varepsilon'(s)) = \Omega \delta_{t,s}$$

We can generate these error terms using the following method (Basu and Lasaridis, 1980).

For the sake of simplicity, let us assume $n = 3$, and we have three observations denoted by $t$. Thus we get three sets of errors.

$$\varepsilon_1(t_1) \quad \varepsilon_1(t_2) \quad \varepsilon_1(t_3)$$

$$\varepsilon_2(t_1) \quad \varepsilon_2(t_2) \quad \varepsilon_2(t_3)$$

$$\varepsilon_3(t_1) \quad \varepsilon_3(t_2) \quad \varepsilon(t_3)$$

From our assumptions we get
$$E(\varepsilon(t_i)) = 0 \quad \varepsilon(t_i)\varepsilon(t_j) = 0 \text{ for } i \neq j$$
$$\varepsilon(t_i)\varepsilon'(t_i) = Q$$

*Step 1*

We arrange the residuals in the following order
$$\varepsilon_1(t_1) \quad \varepsilon_2(t_1) \quad \varepsilon_3(t_1) \quad \varepsilon_1(t_2) \quad \varepsilon_2(t_2) \quad \varepsilon_3(t_2) \quad \varepsilon_1(t_3) \quad \varepsilon_2(t_3) \quad \varepsilon_3(t_3)$$
The variance-covariance matrix for all the sampling period is

$$\begin{bmatrix} \varepsilon_1(t_1) \\ \varepsilon_2(t_1) \\ \varepsilon_3(t_1) \\ \varepsilon_1(t_2) \\ \varepsilon_2(t_2) \\ \varepsilon_3(t_2) \\ \varepsilon_1(t_3) \\ \varepsilon_2(t_3) \\ \varepsilon_3(t_3) \end{bmatrix} [\varepsilon_1(t_1) \; \varepsilon_2(t_1) \; \varepsilon_3(t_1) \; \varepsilon_1(t_2) \; \varepsilon_2(t_2) \; \varepsilon_3(t_2) \varepsilon_1(t_3) \; \varepsilon_2(t_3) \; \varepsilon_3(t_3)]$$

$$= \begin{bmatrix} \varepsilon_1(t_1) \cdot \varepsilon_1(t_1) & \varepsilon_1(t_1) \cdot \varepsilon_2(t_1) & \varepsilon_1(t_1) \cdot \varepsilon_3(t_1) & \cdots & \cdots \\ \varepsilon_2(t_1) \cdot \varepsilon_1(t_1) & \varepsilon_2(t_1) \cdot \varepsilon_2(t_1) & \varepsilon_2(t_1) \cdot \varepsilon_3(t_1) & \cdots & \cdots \\ \varepsilon_3(t_1) \cdot \varepsilon_1(t_1) & \varepsilon_3(t_1) \cdot \varepsilon_2(t_1) & \varepsilon_3(t_1) \cdot \varepsilon_3(t_1) & \cdots & \cdots \\ \cdots & \cdots & \cdots & \cdots & \cdots \\ \cdots & \cdots & \cdots & \cdots & \cdots \\ \cdots & \cdots & \cdots & \cdots & \cdots \end{bmatrix}$$

*Step 2*

We can see three distinctive subcovariable matrices denoted by $Q_1, Q_2, Q_3$ where

$$Q_1 = \varepsilon(t_1)\varepsilon(t_1)$$
$$Q_2 = \varepsilon(t_2)\varepsilon(t_2)$$
$$Q_3 = \varepsilon(t_3)\varepsilon(t_3)$$
$$Q_4 = \varepsilon(t_1)\varepsilon t_2) = Q_6 = 0$$
$$Q_5 = \varepsilon(t_1)\varepsilon(t_3) = Q_8 = 0$$

(Because we assume no correlation between time periods)

$$Q_6 = \varepsilon(t_2)\varepsilon(t_3) = Q_9 = 0$$

We define the covariance matrix of the disturbance as

$$\text{cov}(\varepsilon) = E[\{\varepsilon - E(\varepsilon)\}\{\varepsilon' - E(\varepsilon)'\}]$$
$$= Q$$

Assuming $E(\varepsilon) = 0$ then the above indicates that the covariance matrix $Q$ is the mean of the covariance matrices. In other words

$$Q = \sum_{i=1}^{3} Q_i$$

In this case $Q^{-1}$ exists [if in general $\varepsilon \in E^n$ ($E$ denotes Euclidean spaced) then every $Q_i$ is singular since it consists of $n$ linearly dependent vectors. On the other hand the mean-covariance matrix $Q$ is singular positive definite and thus invertible (i.e. $Q^{-1}$ exists).

*Step 3*

$Q$ is assumed to be positive definite. Then we can decompose $Q$ by a non-singular triangular matrix $P$ such that

$$Q = PP'$$

*Step 4*

Now we can generate a random vector

$$u_t = P \cdot \varepsilon_t, \quad u_t \sim N(0, 1)$$

By construction $E(u_t) = 0$, and $E_t = P^{-1}\mu$

$$\text{cov}(u_t, u_{t'}) = \delta_{tt'} \cdot PIP'$$
$$= \delta_{tt'} \cdot Q$$

when $\delta_{tt'}$ is a Kronecker delta

*Step 5*

After generating the new noise vector $\varepsilon$ for a new period, we have the number of sampling periods as four instead of three. With four periods we have four distinctive sub-matrices (covariance). With these four sub-matrices, we update the mean-covariance matrix $Q$ and then we generate a new set of disturbances. By repeating this method we can generate a vector of residuals for as many periods as we want.

If we incorporate this method to the stochastic control (with certainty equivalence) problem it will create state trajectories which are quite different from the deterministic trajectories, because first we add stochastic error and update the errors depending on the current state. Thus, we incorporate some elements of the closed loop control within the 'certainty equivalence' principle.

**Stochastic control with additive stochastic process**

We consider the stochastic system
$$X(t) = AX(t-1) + BU(t) + C\varepsilon(t)$$

We consider the following performance criterion
$$f = \sum_{t=1}^{N} \{X(t) - X^D(t)\}' Q_x(t) \{X(t) - X^D(t)\}$$
$$+ \sum_{t=1}^{N} \{U(t) - U^D(t)\}' Q_u(t) \{U(t) - U^D(t)\}$$

where $X^D$ and $U^D$ are the policy-maker's desired goal and instrument vector respectively. The weight matrices $Q_X$ and $Q_u$ are symmetric and positive definite.

From the system equation we can obtain (see Basu and Lazaridis, 1983)
$$X(t) = A^t X(0) + \sum_{j=0}^{t-1} A^{t-j-1} BU(j+1) + \sum_{j=0}^{t-1} A^{t-j-1} C\varepsilon(J+1)$$

or

$$X(t) = A^t X(0) + \{A^{t-1} \cdot B, \ldots A \cdot B, B\} \cdot \begin{bmatrix} U(1) \\ U(2) \\ \cdot \\ \cdot \\ \cdot \\ U(t) \end{bmatrix}$$

$$+ \{A^{t-1}, A^{t-2}, \ldots, A, I\} \cdot \begin{bmatrix} W(1) \\ \cdot \\ \cdot \\ \cdot \\ W(t) \end{bmatrix}$$

when $W(i) = C\varepsilon(i)$, $i = 1 \ldots t$

Now we define

$$X = \begin{bmatrix} X(1) \\ \cdot \\ \cdot \\ X(N) \end{bmatrix} ; \quad L = \begin{bmatrix} A \\ A^2 \\ \cdot \\ \cdot \\ A^N \end{bmatrix}$$

$$U = \begin{bmatrix} U(1) \\ \cdot \\ \cdot \\ U(N) \end{bmatrix} ; \quad V = \begin{bmatrix} \varepsilon(1) \\ \cdot \\ \cdot \\ \varepsilon(N) \end{bmatrix}$$

when $X \in E^{Nn}$, $U \in E^{Nm}$, $V \in E^{Nn}$, $L$ is of dimension $Nn \times n$ when $N$ in the total number of time instants considered.

$$\underset{(Nn \times Nn)}{K} = \begin{bmatrix} B & 0 & \ldots & 0 & 0 \\ AB & B & \ldots & 0 & 0 \\ A^{N-1}B & A^{N-2}B & \ldots & AB & B \end{bmatrix}$$

$$\underset{(Nn \times Nn)}{F} = \begin{bmatrix} C & 0 & \ldots & 0 & 0 \\ AC & C & \ldots & 0 & 0 \\ A^{N-1}C & A^{N-2}C & \ldots & AC & C \end{bmatrix}$$

then we can obtain

$$X = LX(0) + KU + FV$$

and the objective function can be written as
$$f = (X - X^D)'Q_1(X - X^D)$$
$$+ (U - U^D)'Q_2(U - U^D)$$

when

$$Q_1 \atop (N_n \times N_n) = \begin{bmatrix} Q_x(1) & & & \\ & Q_x(2) & & \\ & & \ddots & \\ & & & Q_x(N) \end{bmatrix}$$

and

$$Q_2 \atop (N_m \times N_m) = \begin{bmatrix} Q_u(1) & & & \\ & Q_u(2) & & \\ & & \ddots & \\ & & & Q_u(N) \end{bmatrix}$$

Thus
$$f = [LX(0) + KU + FV - X]'Q_1[LX(0) + KU + FV - X^D]$$
$$+ (U - U^D)'Q_2(U - U^D)$$
$$= \left\| \begin{bmatrix} R_1K \\ R_2 \end{bmatrix} U - \begin{bmatrix} R_1X^D - R_1LX(0) - R_1FV \\ R_2U^D \end{bmatrix} \right\|^2$$

when
$$Q_1 = R'_1R_1, Q_2 = R'_2R_2$$

Hence the optimal control level is given by
$$U^* = \begin{bmatrix} R_1K \\ R_2 \end{bmatrix}^+ \cdot \begin{bmatrix} R_1X^D - R_1LX(0) - R_1FV \\ R_2U^D \end{bmatrix}$$

The optimal control sequence above is expressed as a linear combination of the noise involved. The noise vector V can be simulated given the covariance matrix $\Omega$. After a sufficient number of experiments the stochastic path of the control sequence can be approximated from

$$\hat{U}^* = M^{-1} \sum_{j=1}^{M} U^*_j$$

## Case of certainty equivalence

Taking expectation of both sides of the objective function we get

$$Ef = \{LX(0)+KU-X^D\}'Q_1\{LX(0)+KU-X^D\}$$
$$+(U-U^D)'Q_2(U-U^D)+E\{V'F'Q_1FV\}$$

As $U'QU = \text{trace}(Q\lambda)$ where $\lambda = UU'$.

Then $E\{V'F'Q_1FV\} = \text{tr}(F'Q_1FE(VV'))$, which is a constant.

Hence the problem is reduced to a deterministic one and optimal control is given by

$$U^* = \begin{bmatrix} R_1K \\ R_2 \end{bmatrix} \cdot \begin{bmatrix} R_1x^D - R_1LX^D(0) \\ R_2U^D \end{bmatrix}$$

In this method we can obtain optimal control law even though $n < m$, if a minimum norm solution is invoked. Most of the methods for deriving the optimal control law are based on the assumption $n \geq m$ and the speed of the algorithm to coverage is dependent upon the dimension of the control vector. It is particularly restrictive in modelling regional and sectoral economies. If the assumption $n \geq m$ is relaxed, then some of the available methods for optimal control will be inapplicable. The reason is that in almost all of those cases inverse of the matrix $B'QB$ is required ( see Chow, 1975), recalling that $B$ in $n \times m$ and $Q$ is symmetric.

If $m > n$, the increase of $B'QB$ does not exist. Similar reason makes unconstrained optimisation inapplicable. Now if we consider a cost function min $F = \|X - X^D\|^2 \cdot Q$ where $Q$ is a positive definite matrix which can be decomposed such that $Q = R'_1R_1$, the optimal control system which has least norm and minimizes $F$ is given by

$$U^* = \{R_1K\}^+\{R_1X^D - R_1LX(0)\}$$

regardless of the number of state and control variable in the system.

For the perfect measurement case, matrix $K$ is the transmission matrix of the system; controllability assumes that $K$ has full row or column rank dependent upon the number of state and the control variable. Given the properties of matrix $R_1$ it can be verified that for the $(Nn \times Nm)$ rank $(R_1K) = \min(Nn, Nm)$.

This assumes that the pseudo-inverse $(R_1K)^+$ is a right or left inverse of $\{R_1K\}$; from which we can derive that the solution using pseudo-increase is the unique solution.

One may argue that the number of control variables are more than that of the state variables, derivation of a unique solution may also have a mathematical interest since the decision-maker can freely fix paths of some extra control variables. We can say that this may not be always feasible or desirable. In a typical case of a central bank's behaviour one may be left with a large number of controls in the hands of the monetary authorities where the only intention can be to control prices and output; it is not possible for the central bank to fix the trajectories of certain control instruments because in most cases these are highly sensitive. However we may describe this situation as static controllability i.e. instruments are set in such a way that will achieve the targets exactly in every period. A perfect analogue of this situation is a least square regression model where $R^2$ is one and errors are all identically zero (Craine and Havener, 1977).

## Stochastic control with learning (adaptive control)

Certainty equivalence principles are not applicable when uncertainty is embodied within the parametric structure. Stochastic control with active learning is the logical extension to solve these problems. In this framework estimation regarding parameters can be improved over time and the choice of the control trajectories will be influenced by its effects on the parameters. Thus we have to achieve two goals at the same time: optimisation of the system and estimation of the system. We can have an alternative learning process: passive learning when we update the economic system for each time instant and revise our plan accordingly (Chow, 1981). In the case of passive learning we may take into account both parameter covariances and future covariance of the state and control variable of the system. 'If the economic system is bounced around enough by random shocks and/or if the parameter estimates have very narrow confidence intervals at the initial time, then passive learning will be sufficient and there will be little gain with active learning method over passive learning control methods. If on the other hand, confidence bounds are very wide at the initial time and if there are only small natural shocks to the system there can be large gain from using active learning strategies' (Kendrick, 1981).

We elaborate below our method of adaptive control using Bayesian filtering methods (Basu and Lazaridis, 1986), which we have used extensively in the following chapters.

## Stochastic optimal control solution

Suppose our dynamic econometric model can be converted to an equivalent first order dynamic system of the form.

$$x_i = \bar{A}x_{i-1} + \tilde{C}\bar{u}_i + \bar{D}Z_i + \bar{e}_i \qquad (1)$$

When $x_i$ is the vector of endogenous variables, $u_i$ is the vector of control variables, $Z_i$ is a vector of exogenous variables, $e_i$ is the vector of noises which are assumed to be white and gaussian and $A$, $C$ and $D$ are coefficient matrices of proper dimensions (a certain element of $Z_i$ is 1 and corresponds to the constant terms). The parameters of the above system are assumed to be random. Shifting to period $i+1$, we can write

$$x_{i+1} = \bar{A}\bar{x}_i + \bar{C}\bar{u}_{i+1} + \bar{D}\bar{Z}_{i+1} + \bar{e}_{i+1} \tag{2}$$

Now we define augmented vectors and matrices.

$$X_i = \begin{bmatrix} x_i \\ u_i \end{bmatrix}, \quad X_{i+1} = \begin{bmatrix} x_{i+1} \\ u_{i+1} \end{bmatrix}, \quad e_{i+1} = \begin{bmatrix} \bar{e}_{i+1} \\ 0 \end{bmatrix}$$

$$A = \begin{bmatrix} \bar{A} & 0 \\ 0 & 0 \end{bmatrix}, \quad C = \begin{bmatrix} \bar{C} \\ I \end{bmatrix}, \quad D = \begin{bmatrix} \bar{D} \\ 0 \end{bmatrix}$$

So we can rewrite the system as

$$X_{i+1} = AX_i + C\bar{u}_{i+1} + D\bar{Z}_{i+1} + e_{i+1} \tag{3}$$

using the linear advance operator $L^{-1}$, we can write

$$\bar{u}_{i+1} \stackrel{\Delta}{=} L^{-1}\bar{u}_i,$$
$$\bar{Z}_{i+1} \stackrel{\Delta}{=} L^{-1}\bar{Z}_i,$$
$$e_{i+1} \stackrel{\Delta}{=} L^{-1}e_i.$$

Let me define

$$u_i \stackrel{\Delta}{=} L^{-1}\bar{u}_i,$$
$$Z_i \stackrel{\Delta}{=} L^{-1}\bar{Z}_i,$$
$$\varepsilon_i \stackrel{\Delta}{=} L^{-1}e_i.$$

Thus

$$X_{i+1} = AX_i + Cu_i + DZ_i + \varepsilon_i \tag{4}$$

which is a typical linear control system

We can formulate an optimal control problem of the form

$$\min J = \frac{1}{2} \| X_T - \bar{X}_T \|^2 \cdot Q_T + \frac{1}{2} \sum_{i=0}^{T-1} \|X_i - \bar{X}_i\|^2 Q_i. \tag{5}$$

subject to the system (4) described above $T$ indicates the terminal time of the control problem, $Q$ is the weighting matrix and $\bar{X}_i (i = 0, 1, 2, \ldots T)$ is the desired state and control trajectory according to our formulation.

The solution can be obtained according to the minimiZation principle by solving the Ricatti-type equation (see Aström (1970) ).

$$K_T = Q_T \tag{6}$$

$$\Lambda_i = -(E_i C' K_{i+1} C)^{-1} (E_i C' K_{i+1} A) \tag{7}$$

$$K_i = E_i A' K_{i+1} A + \Lambda'_i (E_i C' K_{i+1} A) + Q_i \tag{8}$$

$$h_T = -Q_T X_T \tag{9}$$

$$h_i = \Lambda_i (E_i C' K_{i+1} D) Z_i + \Lambda_i (E_i C') h_{i+1} \tag{10}$$
$$\quad + (E_i A' K_{i+1} D) Z_i + (E_i A)' h_{i+1} - Q_i X_i$$

$$g_i = -(E_i C' K_{i+1} C)^{-1} [(E_i C' K_{i+1} D) Z_i + (E_i C') h_{i+1}] \tag{11}$$

$$X^*_{i+1} = [E_i A + (E_i C) \Lambda_i] X^*_i + (E_i C) g_i + E_i D) Z_i \tag{12}$$

$$u^*_i = \Lambda_i X^*_i + g_i \tag{13}$$

where $u^*_i$ ($i = 0, 1, \ldots, T-1$), the optimal control sequence and $X^*_{i+1}$, the corresponding state trajectory, constitute the solution to the stated optimal control problem.

[In the above equation, $\Lambda_i$ is the matrix of feedback coefficients and $g_i$ is the vector of intercepts. The notation $E_i$ denotes the conditional expectations, given all information up to the period $i$].

Expressions such as $E_i C' K_{i+1} C$, $E_i C' K_{i+1} A$, $E_i C' K_{i+1} A$ are evaluated taking into account the reduced form coefficients of the econometric model and their covariance matrices which are to be updated continuously along with the implementation of the control rules and the control rules should be readjusted accordingly to 'passive learning' methods, however joint densities of matrices $A$, $C$ and $D$ remain constant over the control period.


## Updating method of reduced-form coefficients and their covariance matrices

Suppose we have a simultaneous-equation system.

$$XB' + UT' = R \tag{14}$$

Where $X$ is the matrix of endogenous variable defined on $E^N \times E^n$ and $B$ is the matrix of structural coefficients which refer to the endogenous variables and defined on $E^n \times E^n$. $U$ is the matrix of explanatory variables defined on $e^N \times E^g$ and $\Gamma$ is the matrix of the structural coefficients which refer to the explanatory variables, defined on $E^N \times E^g$. $R$ is the matrix of noises defined on $E^N \times E^n$. We can define matrix $\Pi$ as follows.

$$\Pi = -B^{-1} \Gamma \tag{14a}$$

Goldberger et al (1961) have shown that the asymptotic covariance matrix, say $\Omega$ of the vector $\hat{\Pi}$ which consists of the $g$ columns of matrix $\Pi$ can be approximately by

$$\tilde{\Omega} = \left[\begin{bmatrix}\hat{\Pi}\\I_g\end{bmatrix} \otimes (\hat{B}')^{-1}\right]' F \left[\begin{bmatrix}\hat{\Pi}\\I_g\end{bmatrix} \otimes (\hat{B}')^{-1}\right] \quad (15)$$

where $\otimes$ denotes the Kroneker product $\hat{\Pi}$ and $\hat{B}$ are the estimated coefficients by standard econometric techniques and $F$ denotes the asymptotic covariance matrix of the $n+g$ columns of $(\hat{B}\hat{\Gamma})$ which are assumed to be consistent and asymptotically unbiased estimated of $B\Gamma$

Combining (14) and (14a) we can write

$$X' = \Pi U' + W \quad (16)$$

when $W = B^{-1} R$

Denoting $i^{th}$ column of matrix $X'$ by $x_i$ and the $i^{th}$ column of matrix $W$ by $w_i$, we can write

$$x_i = \begin{bmatrix} U_{1i} & 0 & \ldots & 0 & U_{2i} & 0 & \ldots & 0 & U_{gi} & 0 & \ldots & 0 \\ 0 & U_{1i} & \ldots & 0 & 0 & U_{2i} & \ldots & 0 & 0 & U_{gi} & \ldots & 0 \\ \cdot & \cdot & & \cdot & \cdot & \cdot & & \cdot & \cdot & \cdot & & \cdot \\ \cdot & \cdot & & \cdot & \cdot & \cdot & & \cdot & \cdot & \cdot & & \cdot \\ \cdot & \cdot & & \cdot & \cdot & \cdot & & \cdot & \cdot & \cdot & & \cdot \\ 0 & 0 & \ldots & U_{1i} & 0 & 0 & \ldots & U_{2i} & 0 & 0 & \ldots & U_{gi} \end{bmatrix} \pi + w_i \quad (17)$$

where $u_{ij}$ is the element of $j^{th}$ column and $i^{th}$ row of matrix. The vector $E^{ng}$ consists of the $g$ column of matrix.

Equation (17) can be written in a compact form, as

$$x_i = H_i \pi + w_i, \quad i = 1, 2, \ldots N \quad (17a)$$

where $x_i \in E^n$

$w_i \in E^n$

and matrix $H_i$ is defined on $E^n \times E^{ng}$

In a time-invariant econometric model, the estimated coefficient vector $\hat{\pi}$ is assumed random with constant expectation overtime, so that

$$\pi_{i+1} = \pi_i, \text{ for all } i \quad (18)$$

In a time-varying and stochastic model we can have

$$\pi_{i+1} = \pi_i + \varepsilon_i \quad (18a)$$

where $\varepsilon_i \in E^{ng}$ is the noise.

Considering these, we can rewrite (17a) as

$$x_{i+1} = H_{i+1} \cdot \pi_{i+1} + w_{i+1} \tag{19}$$

$i = 0, 1, \ldots, N-1$

Let us have the following assumptions.

(a) The vector $x_{i+1}$ and matrix $H_{i+1}$ can be measured exactly for $i = 0, 1, \ldots, N-1$.
(b) The noises $\varepsilon_i$ and $w_{i+1}$ are independent discrete white noises with known statistic.

$$E(\varepsilon_i) = 0 \; ; \quad E(w_{i+1}) = 0$$

$E(\varepsilon_i w_{i+1}) = 0$ and $E(\varepsilon \varepsilon') = Q_1 \delta_{ij}$ where $\delta_{ij}$ is the Kronecker delta and $E(w_i w_j) = Q_2 \delta_{ij}$

(c) The state vector is normally distributed with a finite covariance matrix.
(d) $P(\pi_{i+1} \mid \pi_i) = P(\varepsilon_i \mid \pi_i)$
$P(x_{i+1} \mid \pi_{i+1}) = P(w_{i+1} \mid \pi_{i+1})$

Where the above assumptions, the problem set is to evaluate

$$E(\pi_{i+1} \mid x^{i+1}) \triangleq \pi_{i+1}$$

and $\text{cov}(\pi_{i+1} \mid x^{i+1}) \triangleq S_{i+1}$ (the error covariance matrix) where $x^{i+1} = x_1, x_2, x_3, \ldots, x_{i+1}$

**Derivation of the filter**

Given the assumptions above, it is now verified that the conditional probability density function of $\pi_{i+1}$ given $x^{i+1}$ is gaussian and according to Bayes' rule is determined from

$$P(\pi_{i+1} \mid x^{i+1}) = \int P(\pi_i \mid x^i) P(\pi_{i+1}, x_{i+1} \mid \pi_i, x^i) d\pi_i \tag{20}$$

where

$$P(\pi_i \mid x^i) = \text{constant.} \exp\left(-\frac{1}{2} \|\pi_{i+1} - \pi *_i\|^2 S_i^{-1}\right)$$

$\pi *_i \triangleq E(\pi_i \mid x^i), S_i \triangleq \text{cov}(\pi_i \mid x^i)$ ($S_i$ assumed to be invertible)

$$P(\pi_{i+1}, x_{i+1} \mid \pi_i, x^i) = \text{constant.} \exp\left[-\frac{1}{2} \left\| \begin{array}{c} \pi_{i+1} - \pi_i \\ x_{i+1} - H_{i+1}\pi_{i+1} \end{array} \right\|^2_{C_{-1}}\right]$$

$$C = \begin{bmatrix} Q_1 & 0 \\ 0 & Q_2 \end{bmatrix}, \quad C^{-1} \begin{bmatrix} Q_1^{-1} & 0 \\ 0 & Q_2^{-1} \end{bmatrix}$$

Hence

$$P(\pi_{i+1} \mid x^{i+1}) = \text{constant} \int \exp(-\tfrac{1}{2} 1_{J_i}) d\pi_i \qquad (21)$$

where

$$1_{J_i} = (\pi_i - \pi^*_i)' S_i^{-1}(\pi_i - \pi^*_i) + [(\pi_{i+1} - \pi_i)' Q_1^{-1}(\pi_i - \pi_i)] \qquad (22)$$
$$+ (x_{i+1} - H_{i+1}\pi_{i+1})' Q_2^{-1}(x_{i+1} - H_{i+1}\pi_{i+1})$$

We can rewrite (22) as

$$1_{J_i} = (\pi_i - \pi_i^*)' S_i^{-1}(\pi_i - \pi_i^*) + [(\pi_{i+1} - \pi_i^*) - (\pi_i - \pi^*_i)]' \times$$
$$Q_1^{-1}[(\pi_{i+1} - \pi_i^*) - (\pi_i - \pi_i^*)] + [x_{i+1} - H_{i+1}\pi_i^*$$
$$- H_{i+1}(\pi_{i+1} - \pi_i^*)]' Q_2 - 1[(x_{i+1} - H_{i+1}\pi_i^*)$$
$$- H_{i+1}(\pi_{i+1} - \pi_i^*)] \qquad (23)$$

Expanding (23) we can obtain

$$1_{J_i} = (\pi_i - \pi_i^*)' S_i^{-1}(\pi_i - \pi_i^*) + (\pi_{i+1} - \pi_i^*)' Q_1^{-1}(\pi_{i+1} - \pi_i^*)$$
$$- 2(\pi_i - \pi_i^*)' Q_1^{-1}(\pi_{i+1} - \pi_i^*) + (\pi_i - \pi_i^*)' Q_1^{-1}(\pi_i - \pi_i^*)$$
$$+ (x_{i+1} - H_{i+1}\pi_i^*)' Q_2^{-1}(x_{i+1} - H_{i+1}\pi_i^*) - 2(\pi_{i+1} - \pi_i^*)'$$
$$H'_{i+1} Q_2^{-1}(x_{i+1} - H_{i+1}\pi_i^*)$$
$$+ (\pi_{i+1} - \pi_i^*)' H'_{i+1} Q_2^{-1} H_{i+1}(\pi_{i+1} - \pi_i^*) . \qquad (24)$$

and after collecting terms we get

$$1_{J_i} = (\pi_i - \pi_i^*)'(S_i^{-1} + Q_1^{-1})(\pi_i - \pi_i^*)$$
$$+ (\pi_{i+1} - \pi_i^*)'(Q_1^{-1} + H'_{i+1} Q_2^{-1} H_{i+1})(\pi_{i+1} - \pi_i^*)$$
$$- 2(\pi_i - \pi_i^*)' Q_1^{-1}(\pi_{i+1} - \pi_i^*)$$
$$+ (x_{i+1} - H_{i+1} . \pi_i^*)' Q_2^{-1}(x_{i+1} - H_{i+1} . \pi_i^*)$$
$$- 2(\pi_{i+1} - \pi_i^*)' H'_{i+1} . Q_2^{-1}(xi+1 - H_{i+1} . \pi_i^*) \qquad (25)$$

Now define $L_i^{-1} \triangleq (S_i^{-1} + Q_1^{-1})$ and consider the expression

$$2_{J_i} = (\pi_i - \pi_i^*)' L_i^{-1}(\pi_i - \pi_i^*) - 2(\pi_i - \pi_i^*)' L_i L_i^{-1} .$$
$$Q_1^{-1}(\pi_{i+1} - \pi_i^*)$$
$$+ (\pi_{i+1} - \pi_i^*)' Q_1^{-1} L_i L_i^{-1} . L_i . Q_1^{-1}(\pi_{i+1} - \pi_i^*) . \qquad (26)$$

We can rewrite (24) taking into account (25) and (26) as

$$
\begin{aligned}
1_{J_i} = &\ [(\pi_i - \pi_i^*) - L_i Q_1^{-1}(\pi_{i+1} - \pi_i^*)]' L^{-1} \\
& [(\pi_i - \pi^*_i - L_i Q_1^{-1}(\Pi_{i+1} - \pi^*_i)] \\
& + (\pi_{i+1} - \pi_i^*)'(Q_1^{-1} + H_{i+1} Q_2^{-1} H_{i+1} - \\
& Q_1^{-1} L_i Q_1^{-1}(\pi_{i+1} - \pi_i^*) \\
& + (x_{i+1} - H_{i+1}\pi_i^*)' Q_2^{-1}(x_{i+1} - H_{i+1} \cdot \pi_i^*) \\
& - 2(\pi_{i+1} - \pi_i^*)' H'_{i+1} Q_2^{-1}(x_{i+1} - H_{i+1}\pi_i^*)
\end{aligned} \tag{27}
$$

Integration with respect to $\pi_i$ yields

$$
\text{constant} \int \exp(-\tfrac{1}{2} 1_{J_i}) d\pi_i = \text{constant} \exp(-\tfrac{1}{2} 3_{J_i}) \tag{28}
$$

where

$$
\begin{aligned}
3_{J_i} = &\ (\pi_{i+1} - \pi_i^*)'(Q_1^{-1} - Q_1^{-1} L_i Q_1^{-1} + H_{i+1} Q_2^{-1} H_{i+1}) \\
& (\pi_{i+1} - \pi_i^*) + (x_{i+1} - H_{i+1}\pi_i^*)' Q_1^{-1}(x_{i+1} - H_{i+1}\pi_i^*) \\
& - 2(\pi_{i+1} - \pi_i^*)' H_{i+1} Q_2^{-1}(x_{i+1} - H_{i+1}\pi_i^*)
\end{aligned} \tag{29}
$$

Hence

$$
P(\pi_{i+1} / x^{i+1}) = \text{constant} \exp(-\tfrac{1}{2} 3_{J_i}) \tag{30}
$$

Since $P(\pi_{i+1}/x^{i+1})$ is proportional to the likelihood function, by maximizing the conditional probability density function we are also maximizing the likelihood function in order to determine $\pi_{i+1}^*$. Minimization of $3_{J_i}$ is equivalent to maximizing $P(\pi_{i+1}/x^{i+1})$. To minimize $3_{J_i}$, we expand (29) eliminating terms not containing $\pi_{i+1}$ thus obtaining $4_{J_i}$ i.e.

$$
\begin{aligned}
4_{J_i} = &\ \pi'_{i+1}(Q_1^{-1} - Q_1^{-1} L_i Q^{-1} + H'_{i+1} Q_2^{-1} H_{i+1})\pi_{i+1} \\
& - 2\pi'_{i+1}(Q_1^{-1} - Q_1^{-1} L_i Q_1^{-1} + H_{i+1} Q_2^{-1} H_{i+1})\pi_i^* \\
& - 2\pi'_{i+1} H'_{i+1} Q_2^{-1}(x_{i+1} - H_{i+1}\pi_i^*)
\end{aligned} \tag{31}
$$

Differentiating with respect to $\pi'_{i+1}$ and noting that the matrix in the quadratic term is symmetric, one obtains

$$
\begin{aligned}
\partial(4_{J_i})/\partial \pi'_{i+1} = &\ 2(Q_1^{-1} - Q_1^{-1} L_i Q_1^{-1} + H'_{i+1} Q_2^{-1} H_{i+1})\pi_{i+1} \\
& - 2(Q_1^{-1} - Q_1^{-1} L_i Q_i^{-1} + H'_{i+1} Q_2^{-1} H_{i+1})\pi_i^* \\
& - 2H'_{i+1} Q_2^{-1}(x_{i+1} - H_{i+1}\pi_i^*)
\end{aligned} \tag{32}
$$

Equating to zero we get

$$
\begin{aligned}
\pi^*_{i+1} = &\ \pi_i^* + (Q_1^{-1} - Q_1^{-1} L_i Q_1^{-1} + H'_{i+1} Q_2^{-1} H_{i+1})^{-1} \\
& H'_{i+1} Q_2^{-1}(x_{i+1} - H_{i+1}\pi_i^*)
\end{aligned} \tag{33}
$$

Now consider the composite matrix $Q_1^{-1} - Q_1^{-1} L_i Q_1^{-1}$ where

$$L_i \triangleq (S_i^{-1} + Q_1^{-1})^{-1}; \text{ i.e.} \tag{34}$$
$$Q_1^{-1} - Q_1^{-1}(S_i^{-1} + Q_1^{-1})^{-1} Q_1^{-1}$$

According to the matrix identity of Householder (1953) which has the general form $(A + BCB')^{-1} = A^{-1} - A^{-1} B (C^{-1} + B' A^{-1} B)^{-1} B' A^{-1}$, (34) can be written as

$$Q_1^{-1} - Q_1^{-1}(S_i^{-1} + Q_1^{-1})^{-1} Q_1^{-1} = (Q_1 + S_i)^{-1} \triangleq P_{i+1}^{-1} \tag{35}$$

Hence (33) can take the form

$$\pi_{i+1}^* = \pi_i^* + K_{i+1}(x_{i+1} - H_{i+1}\pi_i^*) \tag{36}$$

where

$$K_{i+1} = S_{i+1} H'_{i+1} \cdot Q_2^{-1} \tag{37}$$
$$S_{i+1}^{-1} = P_{i+1}^{-1} + H'_{i+1} Q_2^{-1} H_{i+1} \tag{38}$$
$$P_{i+1}^{-1} = (Q_1 + S_i)^{-1}$$

Matrix $K_{i+1}$ which is defined on $E^{ng} \times E^n$ is identified as the filter gain at the discrete-time instant $i+1$.

In view of the above consideration it is verified that

$$P(\pi_{i+1}/x^{i+1}) = \text{constant} \exp\left[-\frac{1}{2}(\pi_{i+1} - \pi^*_{i+1})' S'_{i+1}(\pi_{i+1} - \pi^*_{i+1})\right]$$

where $\pi^*_{i+1}$ is given by (36).

From (39) it is clear that $P(\pi_{i+1}/x^{i+1})$ is symmetric and unimodal about $\pi^*_{i+1}$ so that all the best estimates, i.e. the conditional mean, the median and mode of $P(\pi_{i+1}/x^{i+1})$ are given by $\pi^*_{i+1}$.

The recursion process is initiated by computing $\pi^*_0$ and $S_0$ from

$$\pi^*_0 = \pi_0 + K_0(X_0 - H_0\pi^*_0) \quad ,$$

where $\pi^*_0 = \hat{\pi}$ i.e. the reduced form coefficients estimated by standard econometric technique and

$$S_0 = (P_0^{-1} + H_0 Q_2^{-1} H_0)^{-1} \tag{40}$$

Applying the matrix identify we get

$$S_0 = P_0 + P_0 H'_0 (Q_2 + H_0 P_0 H'_0)^{-1} \cdot H_0 P_0$$
$$= (I - K_0 H_0) P_0$$

there $K_0 = P_0 H_0 (Q_2 + H'_0 P_0 H_0)^{-1}$ and $P_0 = \Omega$ given by (15)

For the particular problem under consideration $H_0$ is a null matrix, since no observations exist beyond period 1 in the estimation process. The same applies for the vector $x_0$. Accordingly, it is verified that

$$\pi*_0 = \hat{\pi}$$
$$S_0 = P_0 = \Omega$$
$$P_1 = \Omega$$

In cases where the measurement noise vector does not have zero-mean, (36) becomes

$$\pi*_{i+1} = \pi_i* - K_{i+1}(x_{i+1} - H_{i+1}\pi_i* - \bar{w}_{i+1})$$

when $\bar{w}_{i+1} = E(w_{i+1})$

The recursive equation developed in this section can be used to update the reduced form coefficients and their covariance matrix when new information becomes available. At each stage the Ricatti-equation (6) to (13) should be evaluated afresh and optimal controls would be recalculated accordingly. 'Active' control can be obtained after a number of iterations when the solution will move backward and forward to make all calculation regarding optimal controls coverage.

The above methods were used in the subsequent chapter to derive adaptive control solution for the model of the Indian economy.

## Stability

In a Discrete time framework, suppose the time-invariant system is

$$x_{t+1} = Ax_t\,; \quad A \text{ is } n \times n \text{ matrix.}$$

The system is stable if for eigenvalues $(\lambda_i)$ of $A$ are all distinct and if $|\lambda_i| \le 1, i = 1 \ldots n$. The system is asymptotically stable if $A$ has $n$ distinct eigenvalues and if $|\lambda_i| < 1, i = 1 \ldots n$. For further analysis see Kushner (1967) and Aoki (1967).

For a continuous time stochastic system. Consider the stochastic differential equation

$$dx = f(x,t)dt + p(x,t)dw$$

where $x$ denotes the state variables and $w_t$ denotes a normalized vector Weiner process. The real infinitesimal operator $L$ is defined by

$$L = \sum_i f_i(x,t)\frac{\partial}{\partial x_i} + \frac{1}{2}\sum_{ij} S_{ij}(x,t)\frac{\partial^2}{\partial x_i \partial x_j} = \frac{\partial}{\partial t}$$

where

$$S(x,t) = \Big[p(x,t)\Big]\Big[p^T(x,t)\Big]$$

The sufficient condition for exponential asymptotic stability with probability is obtained by Kushner (1965a, 1965b, 1965c, 1967).

## Theorem 1 (Kushner, 1967)

If the stochastic process $x_t$ satisfies the following assumptions:
(i) $V(x)$ is non negative continuous, $V(0) = 0$ and $V(x) \to \infty$ as $\|x\| \to \infty$ where $\|.\|$ is a Euclidean norm. $V(x)$ is defined in the domain of $L$.
(ii) $x_t$ is a right continuous strong Markov process and is uniformly stochastically continuous.
(iii) $L[V(x)] < - DV(x)$ for some $D \geq 0$, then the process $x_t$ is exponentially asymptotically stable in the large with probability one, i.e.

$$P_x \left\{ \sup_{\infty > t \geq T} V(x_t) \geq \lambda \right\} \leq \frac{V(x)\exp(-DT)}{\lambda}$$

where $P_x\{\ldots\}$ is a conditional probability with respect to the initial value $x_0 = x$.

## Controllability

We can mention the following regarding the concept of controllability. If a system can go from the initiable state to the desired state with feasible instruments without violating any of the constraints, the system is controllable. In a time-invariant system the concept can be written as follows.

Suppose the $n$-dimensional system is

$$\dot{x}(t) = Ax(t) + Bw(t).$$

It is completely controllable and and only if the column vectors of the controllability matrix

$$<A|B> \stackrel{\text{def}}{=} (B, AB, \ldots A^{n-1}B) \quad n \times nr \text{ matrix}$$

space the $n$-dimensional matrix $R^n$.

In a discrete time framework if the system is

$$x_{t+1} = Ax_t + Bu_t.$$

We can write

$$x_t = A^t x_0 + Q_t U_{0,t}.$$

Where $Q_t = \left[ A^{t-1}B, A^{t-2}B, \ldots, AB, B \right]$: $n \times tr$ matrix.

$$U_{0,t} = \begin{bmatrix} u_0 \\ u_1 \\ \vdots \\ u_{t-1} \end{bmatrix} \quad : tr - \text{dimensional vector.}$$

The system is completely controllable if rank $Q_t = n$.

If the system is time-varying
$$x_{t+1} = A_t x_t + B_t u_t$$
then
$$x_{t+s} = \phi_{t+s,t} x_t + Q_{t+s,t} U_{t,t+s}$$
where
$$\phi_{t+s,t} = A_{t+s-1} \ldots A_{t+1} \cdot A_t$$

$$Q_{t+s,t} = \begin{bmatrix} \phi_{t+s,t+1} B_t & \phi_{t+s,t+2} B_{t+1} & \ldots & \phi_{t+s,t+s-1} B_{t+s-2} & B_{t+s-1} \end{bmatrix}$$
and
$$U_{t,t+s} = \begin{bmatrix} u_t \\ u_{t+1} \\ \vdots \\ u_{t+s-1} \end{bmatrix}.$$

The system is controllable if and only if
$$\text{rank } (Q_{t+n-1,t}) = n \ .$$

For further discussion see Connors (1967), Bar-Shalom and Sivan (1969).

# 3 Recent advances in macroeconomic policy analysis and the analytical structure of the control model

The derivation of alternative policy structures needs concrete specifications of models. The model should specify 'outcome' in terms of probability distribution over future events in the economy in question for a particular set of policies. The selection of an optimal set of policies needs a specific objective function. This particular description of the problem is valid whether the problem is static or dynamic. In our earlier description current state of the economy is represented by $X_t$ and policy variable $U_t$ should be chosen at period $t$. We can obtain a conditional distribution for $X_{t+1}$ as a function of $X_t$ and $U_t$. The objective function depends on $X_{t+s}$ and on $U_{t+s}$ for a period beyond $t+1$ where $s = 1$ ( where $s = 1 \ldots T$, the terminal time ). Thus we need to set optimal contingency plans for all future dates. In practice we need to review our plans every now and then in order to incorporate new information and problem and forecast possible outcomes of alternative policy structures.

According to the 'Rational Expectation' ($RE$) critique people's choice depends not only on the current values of variable but also on their expectations regarding their future values. Naturally any economic model which disregards people's views about the future and effects of those views on their future actions are of little use for practical policy analysis. It is not sure that people can understand contingency plans for future policy or they will be able to act optimally. Government in most cases announces one set of policies and they don't necessarily follow that same set of policies. 'Rational Expectation' may help us to understand the influence of policy declarations on policy actions, but policy actions may be more influential in shaping people's future actions.

Kydland and Prescott (1977) have observed that under $RE$ optimal policy choice can be time-inconsistent. If a set of contingency plans is chosen at period $t$ for both current and future $X$, the plan for $x_{t+s}$ is not the same as the plan that can be derived if the problem was solved at $t + s$. This is due to the effects of declared policies at period $t$ for period $t + s$. According to Sims

(1982) this criticism may not be correct. A policy can affect people's expectations more prominently through policy actions. A model which ignores the effects is an incorrect model. A correct model should definitely include these effects and will prepare valid conditional projections of the efforts of policy. Control theory can be used in that environment to evaluate policy choices. The problem is to identify the reaction of the public to the policy.

## Response of monetary and fiscal policies under alternative expectation structures: Mathieson model

Mathieson (1978) describes a small economy with perfect capital mobility where the difference between domestic and foreign interest rates is the expected rate of change of exchange rate.

$$r = r^* + \dot{\varepsilon}^e \tag{1.1}$$

where
r = domestic interest rate
r* = world interest rate
$\dot{\varepsilon}^e$ = expected rate of change of the exchange rate

*Monetary policy: adjustment under rational expectations*

Rational expectations are equivalent to perfect foresight i.e. expected rate of change of either the price of domestic goods ($p^e$) or the exchange rate ($\dot{\varepsilon}^e$) will equal the actual rate of change. With adoptive expectations market participants are assumed to adjust to that expectation gradually. Then:

$$\dot{p}^e = \theta(p - p^e) \tag{1.2}$$

$$\dot{\varepsilon}^e = \beta(\varepsilon - \varepsilon^e) \tag{1.3}$$

Money-market equilibrium, in log-normal form, can be expressed as follows.

$$m - \alpha p - (1 - \alpha)P^* - (1 - \alpha)\varepsilon = -\lambda r + \phi y \tag{1.4}$$

Where the left-hand side indicates supply of real balance and the right hand indicates demand for real balance and where $m$, $p$, $p^*$, $\varepsilon$ and $y$ are the logs of the nominal quantity of money, the price of domestic goods, the price of imported goods, the exchange rate and real income. The assumption is that a true price index depends on the price of the domestic goods and the domestic equivalent of the price in imported goods, which will equal the exchange rate multiplied by the price of the imported goods and indicates the weight the price of the domestic goods receives in the general price index.

In the goods market, the demand for the domestic goods ($D$) is taken as a function of the relative price of the domestic goods, the level of real income and the real interest rate.

$$\ln D = \delta(\varepsilon + p* - p) + ry + \sigma[r - \alpha p^e - (1-\alpha)\dot{\varepsilon}^e] \quad (1.5)$$

The real interest rate in equal the nominal interest rate less the expected rate of inflation. The rate of increase in the price of the domestic goods ($\dot{p}$) is assumed to depend on the excess demand for the domestic goods.

$$\dot{p} = \pi\left[\delta(\varepsilon + p* - p) + (r-1)y - \sigma(r - \alpha p^e - (1-\alpha)\dot{\varepsilon}^e)\right] \quad (1.6)$$

If we substitute $\dot{p} = \dot{p}^e$ and $\dot{\varepsilon} = \dot{\varepsilon}^e$ in equation (1.1) to (1.6) we get the following equations.

$$\dot{p} = \{\lambda\delta\pi(\varepsilon + p* - p) - \alpha\delta\pi[m - \alpha p - (1-\alpha)\varepsilon - (1-\alpha)p*\}/(1-\alpha\delta\pi) \quad (1.7)$$

$$\dot{\varepsilon} = -m - \alpha p - (1-\alpha)\varepsilon - (1-\alpha)p*/\lambda - r* - (\phi Y/\lambda) \quad (1.8)$$

A permanent increase in the nominal money supply will create an initial excess supply of real money.

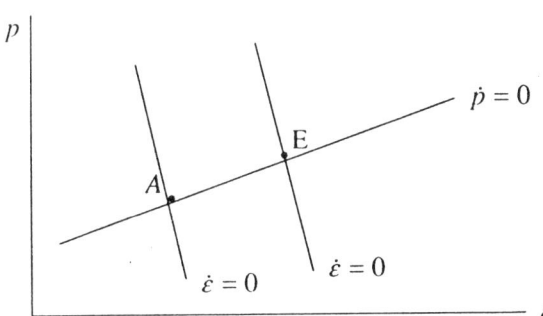

**Figure 3.1 Monetary policy: adjustment under rational expectation**

An increase in $m$ will shift the $\dot{\varepsilon} = 0$ curve to the right but leave the $\dot{p} = 0$ curve unchanged. A higher m will create an excess supply of money which will be offset by a higher $\varepsilon$ for each given value of $p$. Domestic interest rate, according to equation (1.1) can fall below the world interest rate only if there is an expectation that the exchange rate will appreciate over time. This implies that the initial depreciation of exchange rate must be large enough to create the anticipation of a future appreciation. An appreciation will be expected only if the exchange rate depreciates initially by more than the increase in the money supply. This will allow domestic interest rate to decline below the world interest rate. The final movement to the new equilibrium (at point E ) must involve a gradual increase in the price of domestic goods. The final movement towards E involve a gradual increase in the price of the domestic goods and a gradual appreciation of the exchange rate.

The adjustment process under rational expectation includes an initial depreciation of the exchange rate coupled with no change in the price of the domestic goods and then an appreciation of the exchange rate associated with a rising price of the domestic goods.

## Monetary policy: adjustment under adaptive expectations

Under adaptive expectation, both the expected price of the domestic goods and the expected exchange rate will be fixed during the initial period. This reflects that expectation respond only slowly to actual price movements. Under adaptive expectations, the adjustment process will be described by equations (1.1) – (1.4) and (1.6).

$$r = r^* + \varepsilon^e$$
$$\dot{p}^e = \alpha(P - P^e)$$
$$\dot{\varepsilon}^e = \beta(\varepsilon - \varepsilon^e)$$
$$m - \alpha p - (1-\alpha)p^* - (1-\alpha)\varepsilon = -\lambda r + \phi y$$
$$\dot{p} = \pi[\delta(\varepsilon + p^* - p) + (r-1)y - \sigma[r - \alpha \dot{p}^e - (1-\alpha)\dot{\varepsilon}^e]]$$

An increase in $m$ will create an initial excess supply of money. To eliminate the portfolio imbalance, the private sector will buy bonds and generate capital outflow. However as long as the expected rate remains fixed, asset market arbitrage will hold domestic interest rate down to the world interest rate. The private sector can therefore initially purchase bonds in the world market at a fixed nominal interest rate. This capital outflow will lead to discrete depreciation of the spot exchange rate. In the diagram, the increase in the money supply will shift the EE curve to the right, but $\dot{p} = 0$ curve will be unchanged.

The initial depreciation of the exchange rate will lead the private sector to increase the estimate of the expected exchange rate ($\dot{\varepsilon}^e > 0$). Along with this, asset market arbitrage will force the domestic interest rate above the world interest rate. The initial depreciation of the exchange rate will drive up the price of domestic goods, so for some time there will be a rising price level and a rising domestic interest rate.

The interaction between changes in actual and expected exchange rate and price level movement means that the economy can follow either a cyclical or direct path to its new long-run equilibrium involving a higher $p$ and $\varepsilon$.

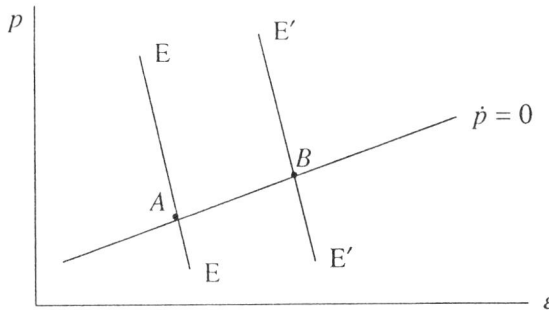

**Fig 3.2 Fiscal policy: adjustment under rational expectations**

In this model the government spending is expressed as a proportion ($g$) of private spending ($D$). The tax revenue is raised as a lump sum and a tax on income. Bonds will finance any deficit in public budgets. As a result we get the public budget constraint as

$$dB^G/dt = gPD + rB^G - t_0 - t_1 pY \tag{1.9}$$

when $B^G$ = the stock of government bonds
$t_0$ = lump sum taxes
$t_1$ = income tax rate
Nominal Disposable income is defined as

$$Y_D = pY + rB^D + rB^F - t_0 - t_1 pY \tag{1.10}$$

Tax rate and bond sales will impute for the effects of fiscal policy on the asset market. Changes in public expenditure and disposable income will produce effects of fiscal policies on the goods market. Condition for the money market will be the same as that in Fig 4. If we assume that the government spending ($G$) can be expressed as a proportion of private spending on domestic goods, the total demand for domestic goods will be
$G + D = gD + D = (1 + g)D$.
Equation (1.6) can be rewritten as

$$\dot{p} = \pi(ln(1+g) + \delta(\varepsilon + p^* - p) - \sigma(r - \alpha\dot{p}^e - \alpha\dot{p}^e) + ry_D - y).$$

Under 'rational expectation', government bond sales will go up to finance public expenditure. If the government bonds are sold abroad, capital flows can create an expected exchange rate appreciation. That will lead to increased money demand as a result of domestic interest rate going below the world interest rate. If the nominal money supply is fixed, general price level will decline so as to increase real money supply. That is possible if there is an appreciation to exchange rate.

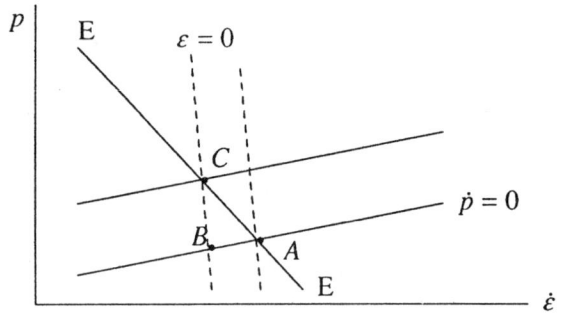

**Fig 3.3 Adjustment under adaptive expectations**

In the diagram, an increase in $g$ will raise the $\dot{p} = 0$ curve but $\dot{\varepsilon} = 0$ curve will not change. Increased government spending will increase excess demand in the domestic market which can be eliminated by increased price level at each level of exchange rate. The initial appreciation of the exchange rate is given by the movement from $A$ to $B$. However, higher level of government spending will increase domestic price which will reduce real supply of money. In order to maintain money market equilibrium, price of imported goods should be reduced by appreciation of the exchange rate.

Under 'adaptive expectation', the announcement of an increase in the level of government spending will have no initial impact on the level of exchange rate, the price of domestic goods or the domestic interest rate. The effects of an increase in government expenditure will be much slower under adaptive expectations than under rational expectations. In the medium term the initial excess demand for domestic goods will drive up the prices and real supply of money will be reduced. Thus the price of imported goods should go down and as a result exchange rate will then be appreciated. That will lower the expected volume of the exchange rate and the domestic interest rate will go down with respect to the world interest rate.

In the light of the above discussion we can compare alternative paths, $r$, $p$ and $e$ under rational and adaptive expectations and we can obtain the following result from the Mathieson Model.

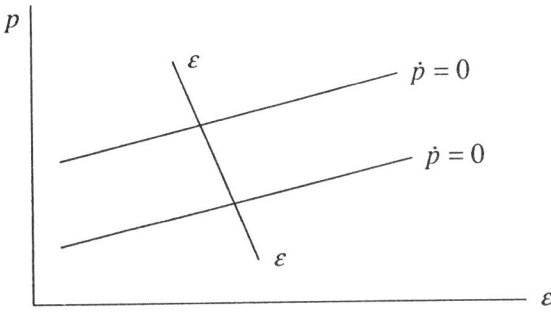

**Fig 3.4 Adjustment under adaptive expectations**

## Monetary policy

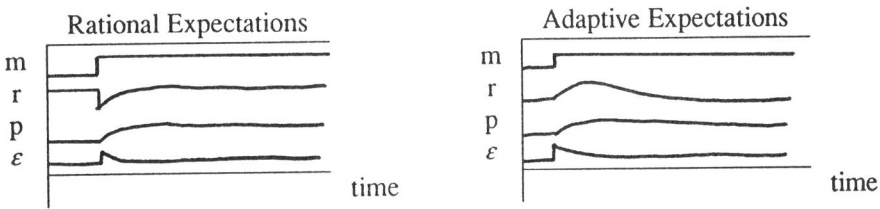

## Fiscal policy

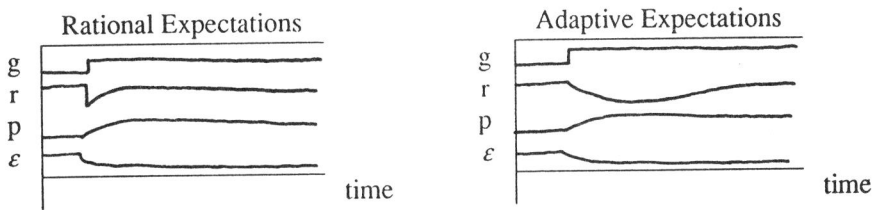

**Fig 3.5 Comparison of rational an adaptive expectations**

As we can see in the case of fiscal policy the difference between the rational expectations and adaptive expectations are only in the speed of adjustments. However in the case of monetary policy, interest rate under rational expectations will behave differently than under adaptive expectations.

## Rules verses discretion

The issues regarding best monetary policy regimes can be categorised into three paths: a) debate between monetary rules and discretionary regime; b) debate regarding the best rule and c) debates regarding their implementations. Following Barro (1983) Alesina (1988) had formulated a simple model to address this issue. Consider an economy with no capital described by a simple supply function with constants set equal to zero and parameter set equal to one.

$$y_t = \pi_t - w_t + \varepsilon_t \qquad (2.1)$$

When $y_t$ is the output, $w_t$ is the rate of growth of nominal wage, and $\varepsilon_t$ is the disturbance term with $\bar{\varepsilon}_t = 0$ and $\sigma_\varepsilon^2$ is known, and $\pi_t$ is the rate of inflation.

$$w_t = \pi_t^e = E(\pi_t/I_{t-1}) \qquad (2.2)$$

When $I_{t-1}$ is the information set available at $(t-1)$ and E is the expectation operator. Suppose the central bank minimizes a quadratic loss function defined on inflation and output, given in each period by

$$C = \{(1/2)\pi_t^2 + (b/2)(y_t - k)^2\} \qquad (2.3)$$

With $k > 0$ and $b > 0$ ; $k$ is the largest level of output. Discretionary policy implies minimization of $C$ with respect to the constraint imposed by (2.2) where as 'rules' implies unconstrainted minimization of $C$. It is possible to show unconstrained minimization of $C$ from (2.3) will give us the following rule

$$\pi_t^R = -(b/(1+b))\varepsilon_t \qquad (2.4)$$

At the same time constrained minization of $C$ from (2.3) given (2.1) and (2.2) will give the discretionary policy.

$$\pi_t^D = b_k - (b/(1+b))\varepsilon_t \qquad (2.5)$$

The extra term $b_k$ in (2.5) implied the inflationary bias by the lack of binding commitments. The best uncontingent rule in the above example is

$$\pi^{SR} = 0 \qquad (2.6)$$

when SR means "simple rule". It is possible to show that

$$C^R < C^{SR} \text{ and } C^R < C^D \qquad (2.7)$$

$$C^D < C^{SR} \text{ iff } K^2(1+b) < \sigma\varepsilon^2 \qquad (2.8)$$

So 'discretion' is best feasible alternative if (a) a 'rule' cannot be implemented; (b) the inequality of (2.8) holds. In a period of high instability, when $\sigma_\varepsilon^2$ will be high enough, the inequality (2.8) is satisfied and a 'simple' monetary rule is inferior to a discretionary policy. Flood and Isard (1989) has proved a mixed strategy of rule and discretion can be the best alternative under certain conditions.

**Proximate targets**

The assumption that the monetary authority exercises perfect control over the money supply and the interest rate amounts to assuming that they are instruments of monetary policy. In reality there are intermediate targets to be controlled by open-market operations, reserve requirement changes and discount rate changes. The notion that the monetary authority should focus on manipulating a proximate target variable such as the interest rate or the money supply rests on the validity of the assumption that open market operations can be used to move the interest rate or money supply in a desired direction. A fundamental assumption is that open market purchases push the interest rate down and increase the money supply. If the assumption does not hold, then the usefulness of the variable as intermediate target is open to question.

Waud (1973) had demonstrated that the effect of high powered money on interest rate is indeterminate. The analysis is as follows. Suppose the total net wealth of the private sector of the economy is assumed to consist of three assets: high powered or outside money defined as the sum of member bank deposits at the central reserve bank plus currency, equity shares $a$ and government bonds $B$ whose prices an equal to the reciprocal of the nominal rate of interest. The real value of equity shares is the capitalised value of all business profits

$$a = \pi \frac{(Y)}{r} \qquad (2.1.1)$$

when $r$ is the real rate of interest, $\pi(Y)$ is business profits assumed to be an increasing function of the real output level $Y$. Net real private wealth $w$ is then

$$w = \frac{B}{r} + a + H \qquad (2.1.2)$$

when $H$ is the real value of high powered money, $r$ is the real rate of interest and $B$ is the number of government bonds held by the private sector.

$$M_d = M(r, w, y, A) \qquad (2.1.3)$$

given the demand for money balances, when $A$ is an exogenous shift parameter. Assuming a fractional reserve banking system, the money supply is

$$M_S = Hh(r) \qquad (2.1.4)$$

when $1 < h(r) < \frac{1}{b}$, $b$ is the legal reserve requirement against demand deposits.

The money market equilibrium requires $M_d = M_s$, thus

$$M(r, \frac{B}{r} + \frac{\pi(Y)}{r} + H, Y, A) - Hh(r) = 0 \qquad (2.1.5)$$

The commodity market equilibrium demands investment savings equality, then

$$I(r, Y, E) = s(r, w, Y) \qquad (2.1.6)$$

when E is an exogenous shift parameter.

In the case of open market operations, the increase in the quantity of high powered money in circulation is equal to the amount expanded on the purchase of bonds.

$$dH = - dB/r \qquad (2.1.7)$$

Totally differentiating equation (2.1.5) and (2.1.6) with respect to $Y, r, H$ and $B$, eliminating $B$ from the result by using (2.1.7), and solving for $\frac{dY}{dH}$ and $\frac{dr}{dH}$ gives

$$\frac{dY}{dH} = -\frac{1}{\Delta} h(r) \left[ \frac{dI}{dr} - \frac{dS}{dr} + \frac{dS}{dw}(B + \pi(Y)) \frac{1}{r} \right] > 0 \qquad (2.1.8)$$

$$\frac{dr}{dH} = \frac{1}{\Delta} h(r) \left[ \frac{dI}{dY} - \frac{ds}{dN}\frac{d\pi}{dY} - \frac{dS}{dY} \right] \gtrless 0 \qquad (2.1.9)$$

when

$$\Delta = \begin{vmatrix} [I_2 - S_2 \frac{\pi Y}{r} - S_3][I_1 - S_1 + S_2(B + \pi(Y))\frac{1}{r}] \\ [M_2 \frac{\pi Y}{r} + M_3][M_1 - M_2(B + \pi(Y))\frac{1}{\gamma} - Hhr] \end{vmatrix}$$

when

$$I_1 = \frac{dI}{dr} > 0, I_2 = \frac{dI}{dY} > 0, \; S_1 = \frac{dS}{dr} > 0;$$

$$S_2 = \frac{dS}{dw} < 0, S_3 = \frac{dS}{dp} > 0, \; y = \frac{d\pi}{dY} > 0 \text{ and } \Delta > 0$$

Because the sign of (2.1.9) is ambiguous it is not possible to say what ultimate effect an open-market operation will have on the interest rate. Thus it is not clear that the monetary authority can move the interest rate in the predictable directions. This situation seems to violate an eminently reasonable and necessary prerequisite for any variable to be used as an intermediate target of monetary policy. Attempts to achieve or maintain the ultimate target of full employed or real income, by focusing on the proximate target variable, the interest rate or the money supply may lead to inconsistencies with the ultimate goal. The solution to this problem is to achieve empirical estimate of the responses and to focus attention to the ultimate targets regarding real income etc with the help of realistic investments.

## Fiscal instruments: interrelations with monetary instruments

Interrelations between fiscal and monetary policies are quite obvious. Fiscal deficits add to the money supply and government bond sales (or purchases) are related to the money supply. The government can earn revenues domestically through taxation, bond sales and borrowing from the central bank (which is directly related to the money supply procedures). The level of public debt (the gap between public revenue and earnings) can influence interest rate and money market significantly.

Recent literature on fiscal policies (see Tanzi, 1977; Miller, 1982; Buiter, 1983; Spaventa, 1989, Rodriguez, 1978; McCallum, 1984; Calvo, 1985; Masson, 1985) are mainly on impacts of public deficit and debts on the macroeconomics and on the sustainability of the deficit and debt when the economy is under pressure from inflation (which can very well be the result of public deficit and debt). That part of interest payments that simply reflects the erosion of the principal as a consequence of inflation constitutes, therefore, an implicit repayment of the principal. This may be the same as amortization payment, however it may be treated as government expenditures which can add to the deficit. Bondholder may reinvest those proceeds in additional government bonds at existing market conditions. In this case, the conventional measure of deficit is likely to overstake the aggregate demand effect of the deficit of the economy.

If we define current account deficit ($CA$) as $CA = D_G + D_P$ when $D_p$ is the private sector's net balance and $D_G$ is the government fiscal deficit (which is defined as $D_G = G + I - T$, where $G$ is nominal government expenditure including the real components of interest payments, $I$ * stands for the monetary correction and T is current tax and nontax revenue). The current account deficit ($CA$) equal the fiscal deficit $D_G$ when private sector is in balance ($D_p = 0$).

If there is any inflation, an increase in public sector deficit caused by an increase in interest payments (which compensates for inflation) would raise the private sector surpluses by equivalent magnitude if those payments are fully reinvested in public bonds. In this case there will not be any impact on

---

* $I$ can be defined as accrued increase in the nominal value of indexed debt, if such increase is treated as a deficit-determining expenditure.

the current account, so the increase in the public sector deficit is unlikely to result in further demand pressures.

We can define $D_G$ and $D_p$ in the following way regarding their financing

$$D_G = F_G + \Delta M^s + \Delta B^s$$
$$D_p = F_p - \Delta M^D - \Delta B_D$$

when $F_G$ = Foreign financing to the public sector
$F_p$ = Foreign financing to the private sector
$\Delta B^s$ = net increase in domestic government borrowing
$\Delta M^s$ = (nominal) increase in the supply of base money
$\Delta M^D$ = increase in private sector's money holdings
$\Delta B^D$ = increase in holdings of government bonds

$$\text{If } F_G = 0 = F_p, \ CA = D_G - M^D - B^D \tag{3.1}$$

then if
$$\Delta M^D = 0, \ CA = D_G - B^D$$
$$= G + I - T - B^D$$
$$= (G - T) + (I - B^D) \tag{3.2}$$

Equation (3.1) indicates that changes in the conventionally defined deficit will affect current account only if those changes are not matched by changes in the same direction in the nominal demand for either money or government bonds.

Equation (3.2) indicates that the higher deficit may not have any current account implication if higher inflation induced interest payment $I$ is matched equally by an increase in the nominal holdings of bonds.

Thus inflation, by creating the possibility of a significant relationship between increases in government deficits and increases in private sectors demand for bonds, weakens the link between budget deficit and current account. In general, there is a strong presumption that the fiscal deficit will influence current account developments when a country's foreign financing possibilities are opened. When foreign financing becomes tight and foreign reserves are exhausted, the size of the current account deficit may be limited. Inflation may then become the main consequence of fiscal deficits. In those conditions, the re-financeability of the inflationary service of the public debt reduces the need to either foreign financing or monetization of deficits without crowding the private sector out of financial markets.

Sustainability of fiscal deficits and debt is an important issue (see Mason, 1989, Spaventa, 1989). Keynes (1923) had pointed out that "the ability or the willingness of a government to collect a rising amount of taxes is likely to set a limit to rationale debt growth. Keynes had suggested two remedies - a capital levy or monetization for the purpose of reducing the real value of debt.

## Fiscal rules and intertemporal budget constraint

Spaventa's (1989) analysis has derived the relationship between debt, tax rule and monetary policies. We can define government's borrowing requirement ($F$) in the following way

$$F_t = G_t + iB_t - T_t$$

where $G$ is the government expenditure, $B$ is the stock of one-period bonds issued at par, $T$ is the taxes and i the nominal rate of interest on bonds. Thus

$$f_t = g_t + ib_t - \tau_t \tag{4.1}$$

where

$$f_t = F_t/Y_t; \quad b_t = B_t/Y_t; \quad \tau_t = T_t/Y_t$$

Similarly if $m$ takes into account the financing of public deficit

$$F_t = \dot{B}_t + \dot{M}_t - (n_t + p_t)B_t$$

where $n_t$ is the real growth rate of $Y_t$ and $P_t$ is the rate of inflation. Thus

$$f_t = \dot{b}_t + \dot{M}_t/Y_t - (n_t + p_t)b_t \tag{4.2}$$

Suppose the real rate of interest ($r$) = $i_t - p_t$ and monetary financing of the deficit is the only source of increase of base money. We also assume that base money will grow at the rate equal to the rate of growth of real GDP and the inflation rate; i.e.

$$\pi_t = n + p_t$$

and

$$\dot{M}/Y = \lambda_t.(M_t/Y_t)$$
$$= \lambda_t.m_t$$

combining (4.1) and (4.2) and the above assumption we can write

$$\dot{b}_t = g_t - \tau_t + (i_t - n - p_t)b_t - \dot{M}_t/Y_t$$
$$= g_t - \tau_t + (r - n)b_t - \lambda_t m_t \tag{4.3}$$

Equation (4.3) can be integrated to derive the inter-temporal budget constraint.

$$b_t = \int_t^\infty \tau_s \, e^{-(r-n)(s-t)} \, ds + \int_t^\infty \lambda_s m_s e^{-(r-n)(s-t)} \, ds$$

$$- \int_t^\infty g_s e^{(e-r-n)(s-t)} \, ds + \lim(s \to \infty) \, b_s e^{-(r-n)(s-t)} \qquad (4.4)$$

Given a fiscal rules respect of the intertemporal budget constraint determines the behaviour of taxation, the existence of a limit to the tax burden may make the rule unsustainable after a certain time. That is contrary to the recently rediscovered "Ricardian - equivalence theorem" (Ricardo, 1951; Buchanan, 1958; Barro, 1974, 1978), according to which under a specific set of circumstances it actually makes no difference to the level of aggregate demand throughout the economy if the government finances its outlays by debt/or by taxation. (This foreign path of expenditures, it is economically equivalent to maintain a balanced budget or to run a debt financed deficit since the substitution of debt for taxes does not affect private sector wealth and consumption.) The issue of public debt in the current period is always accompanied by a planned increase in future tax collections which would be needed to serve this higher level of public indebtedness.

Suppose we consider a two period model, where period 0 is the 'present' and period 1 is the 'future'. The government budgets for period 0 and 1 are given in nominal terms by

$$G_0 - \tau_0 + i_{-1} B_{-1} = (B_0 - B_{-1}) + M_0 - M_{-1}) \qquad (4.5)$$

$$G_1 - \tau_1 + i_0 B_0 = -B_0 + (M_1 - M_0) \qquad (4.6)$$

where period 1 reflects historically given conditions. Government budget deficits can be financed by issuing debtor money. Expressing this equation in real terms we can obtain:

$$g_0 + g_1(1+r_0)^{-1} + (1+r_{-1})b_{-1} + (1+\pi_0)^{-1}m_{-1}$$
$$= \tau_0 + \tau_1(1+r_0)^{-1} + (i_0/(1+i_0)) \, m_0 + m_1(1+r_0)^{-1} \qquad (4.7)$$

when

$$1 + \pi_0 = P_0/P_{-1}$$

Equation (4.7) is the intertemporal government budget constraints similarly intertemporal budget constraint of the private sector is given by

$$C_0 + C(1+r_0)^{-1} + (i_0 m_0)(1+r_0)^{-1} + m(1+r_0)^{-1}$$
$$= y_0 + y_1(1+r_0)^{-1} - \tau_0 - \tau_1(1+r_0)^{-1} + m_{-1}(1+\pi_0)^{-1} - (1+r_{-1})b'_{-1}$$
$$(4.8)$$

and $C_0$ and $C_1$ are the real private consumption for the period 0 and period 1 respectively, and $b_1$ is the private sector debt.

Combining (4.7) and (4.8) we can obtain

$$C_0 + C_1(1 + r_0)^{-1} = (y_0 - g_0) + (1 + r_0)^{-1}(y_1 - g_1) \qquad (4.9)$$

assuming a debtor position of the public sector must be matched by a creditor position of the private sector $b' = -b$.

Equation (4.9) in the intertemporal budget constraint of the private sector. Thus, any two government policy patterns $(g_0, g_1, M_0, M_1, \tau_0, \tau_1)$ and $(g_0, g_1, M_0, M_1, \tau_0, \tau_1)$ that satisfy in intertemporal government budget constraint induce the same behaviour by the private sector because the policy changes cannot affect private sector budget sets (Lucas (1984)).

However, there are possible cases when the Ricardian equivalence theorem may not work. Leiderman and Blejer (1989) have analysed several cases e.g. the existence of borrowing constraints, of distortionary taxes, of uncertainty about future taxes and of different planning horizons for private and public sectors. Even if the tax burden is unlimited, the intertemporal budget constraint is not sufficient to establish a sustainability rule of public debt if debt can affect the real interest rate. This is more likely if the expectation of approaching unsustainability may cause a demand for risk premium on government bonds. Even when the real growth rate of the economy exceeds the real interest rate, debt should not be allowed to grow given a fiscal regime because that favourable situation may not perpetuate. Growth rate can go down or real cost of debt may go up due to some exogenous factor: at the same time it may be difficult to revise a given fiscal regime.

**Policy models for growth and adjustment**

Financial stability and growth are the pressing problem for any policy framework. Khan and Montiel (1989; see also Khan, Montiel and Hague, 1990, 1986) have proposed a model which is in the spirit of the IMF-world Bank induced adjustment programme for the developing countries. The analytical structure of the model is a combination of neoclassical growth model and the monetary approach to balance of payments. Khan's model is an extension and synthesis of earlier models developed within the IMF, the most famous of these is Polak model (Polak 1957) which is as follows.

*Polak model*

The model composed of the basic parts: real economy, monetary sector and the balance of payments.

*Real Economy*

$$Y = P \cdot \bar{Y} \tag{5.1}$$

GDP is determined exogenously by real GDP ($\bar{Y}$) when $P$ is the domestic price level.

*Monetary sector*

$$\Delta M = \Delta M^S = \Delta M^D$$
$$= (1/v)\Delta Y \tag{5.2}$$

The money market is in flow equilibrium and demand for money following simple quantity theory, $v$ is the velocity of circulation.

*Balance of payments*

$$\Delta R = (X - Z) - \Delta F_p - \Delta F_G \tag{5.3}$$

When $\Delta R$ is the change in the foreign exchange reserve, i.e. balance of payment surplus which consists of trade surplus between export ($X$) and imports ($Z$) and private sector's net accumulation of foreign assets ($F_p$) and public sectors net accumulation of foreign ($F_G$). Exports ($X$) and capital flows ($\Delta F = \Delta F_p + \Delta F_G$) are exogenous, whereas imports ($Z$) is endogenous, as a function of nominal GDP ($Y$).

$$z = aY \tag{5.4}$$

The basic constraints of the model are as follows.

*Private sector's budget constraint*

The private sector owns all factors of production. The sale of current output generates nominal income ($Y$). It can borrow ($\Delta D_p$) from the banking system. Thus the budget constraint is

$$Y + \Delta D_p = T + C_p + \Delta K + \Delta M + \Delta F_p \tag{5.5}$$

$T$ is the tax, $C_p$ is the private sector's consumption, $\Delta K$ is investment, $\Delta M$ is the monetary assets.

*Public sector's budget constraint*

The public sector receives taxes and does not do any investment, it can borrow from the banking system. Thus the budget constraint is

$$T + \Delta D_G = C_g + \Delta F_G \tag{5.6}$$

when $C_G$ is the public consumption.

*Banking sector's budget constraint*

The central bank as a financial intermediary acquires assets ($\Delta R$, $\Delta D_p$ and $\Delta D_G$) and liabilities ($\Delta M$). Thus the constraint is

$$\Delta M = \Delta R + \Delta D_p + \Delta D_G \tag{5.7}$$

*Khan model*

Khan et al (1990, 1989, 1981) have proposed an extension of the Polak model. The original Polak model has no explanation regarding real output ($Y$), the exchange rate was unrelated to the rest of the economy, Khan et al have corrected this two features by introducing new relationships which are as follows.

*Real output*

$$\Delta Y = \rho^{-1}(\Delta K/(1 + \Delta P)) \tag{5.1.1}$$

Thus the real output is determined by $\rho$ (incremental capital-output ratio) and real investment (nominal investment $\Delta K$ deflated by the aggregate price $P$).

*Price level*

Aggregate price $P$ is related to the domestic price ($P_D$) and the exchange rate ($e$) in the following way

$$\Delta P = (1 - \alpha)\Delta P_D + \alpha \Delta e$$

$\alpha$ is the share-coefficient.

*Exports*

Exports ($X$) now depends on both domestic price ($P_D$) and the exchange rate.

$$X = X_{-1} + (X_{-1} + C)\Delta e + C\Delta P_D$$

*Imports*

Imports ($Z$) also depends on income ($Y$) and domestic price ($P_D$) and the exchange rate ($e$)

$$Z = Z_{-1} + (Z_{-1} - b)\Delta e + b\Delta P_D + a\Delta Y$$

Thus in the Khan model we have three targets; real income growth ($\Delta Y^*$), domestic price inflation ($\Delta P_D^*$) and balance of payment surplus ($\Delta R^*$) and we have the following instruments

$T$ or $C_G$, $\Delta D_p$, $\Delta_G$ and $\Delta e$

The basic problem of the Khan model is the indeterminacy. Suppose the government is controlling the economy i.e. $T$, $\Delta D_g$ and $\Delta e$, the question is $\Delta D_p$ will be uncontrolled and as a result targets $Y^*$, $\Delta P_D^*$ and $\Delta R^*$ cannot be reached. Suppose $D_p$ can be controlled the market rate of interest which in turn can be controlled by the central bank's discount rate, $C_p$ will be uncontrolled and as a result the private sector's budget constraint may not be satisfied. Also the assumption that the private sector owns all factors of production is an unrealistic assumption for most developing countries when government leads the way. In view of the situation an alternative model can be developed.

## Alternative policy analysis: analytical structure of the econometric model

In section 5 above, we have analysed the IMF-World Bank induced model for structural adjustments for the developing countries which assumes away any role for the public sector in the generation of national output and investment. So in effect structural adjustment means abolition of public sector and to introduce a complete capitalistic economy. There is no guarantee that this experiment can bring any sustainable stability and growth for the developing countries, in fact the performances of the countries in Africa who are going through the adjustment programme for nearly a decade are far from success. The prevailing economic structure of the countries who are not so much dependent on the IMF, is a mixed one, i.e. public sector plays a significant role in the generation of national output and investment. The econometric model described in the subsequent chapters follows the idea of a mixed economy with national planning authority trying to give a desired direction to the private sector, so that the combined effort of the private and the public sector will achieve the planned target. This proposed structure is certainly more realistic and less ideologically motivated than the structure proposed by the IMF.

In a mixed economy, planning has to take into account how the private sector formulates and revises its expectation regarding various exogenous factors like international price and weather, as well as government policies and their possible impacts on the endogenous variables (or target variables) in the economy. Normally the government formulates its plan for the public sector and also sets the limit for the private sector over the next five years. The government can regulate the private sector by various means, such as licences, investment quotes, tax-subsidy rates, bank interest rates and by various monetary controls.

The private sector, knowing the targets of the government, formulates its own expectations regarding the fulfilments of these targets (because it never expects that the government can fulfil its targets exactly) and possible movement of various policy instruments. It behaves according to its expectations and the realization of past expectations and thus allocates its resources. So the optimum design of the government monetary-fiscal policies should be to help the private sector to move towards the desired directions (as defined by the planners) taking into account private sector's expectation. The purpose of monetary and public financial policies in such an environment should be to formulate different central bank policies, such as statutory reserve ratio and liquidity ratios for the commercial banks, the government discount rate and the net domestic credit expansion, so that the private sector would react in the desired way given the desired goal of the physical planners regarding national income, balance of payments, domestic adsorptions and prices.

Private sector's expectations change according to policies declared by the physical planners and the policies expected to be followed by the central bank. The central bank should in order to derive an optimum sets of policies, take into account these expectation – structures and revise their policies. The following analysis will describe the analytical structure of the model whereas in the subsequent chapter will derive optimum paths for various monetary instruments so as to achieve these objectives.

The chief responsibility of the monetary authority is to examine the impacts of different monetary controls on the behaviour of the private sector and to foresee the future course of action of the private sector in anticipation of these monetary policies. The model accepts the definition of balance of payments and money stock according to the "monetary" approach but without any explicit investment or consumption function. The reason is that private investment was publicly controlled by various means of licences and quotas and it is the planning commission who ultimately used to decide the nature and the composition of private investment. The consumption of essential commodities for the poorer section of the population was controlled by the government, although not fully. Non-essential consumption was restricted by various government tax and subsidy policies. Hence the normal neoclassical or Keynesian type private investment or consumption function will not reflect the true nature of the controlled mixed economy. The domestic adsorption can reflect the combined response of both private and public investment and consumption to the planned target for national income set by the planning commission and to the various market forces reflected in the market interest rate and exchange rate. The market interest rate can be influenced by the central bank discount rate, but is ultimately determined by the market. The exchange rate under managed floating system does fluctuate according to the influences of the balance of payment deficits or surpluses, reflecting demands and supplied of foreign exchange. The analytical structure of the model is as follows (a related version was published in Basu (1986)).

## Absorption function and national income

Domestic absorption reflects the behaviour of both the private and public sector regarding both consumption and investment. Although the net investment per year incorporates an ever increasing participation by the public sector but in the economy as a whole the importance of the private sector is still paramount (mainly because of the great importance of the agricultural sector). Domestic real adsorption is influenced by real national income, market interest rate and foreign exchange rate. We assume a linear relationship.

$$(A/P)_t = a_0 + a_1(Y/P)_t - a_2(IR)_t - a_3 EXR_t \qquad (6.1)$$

The relation between the national income and adsorption can be defined as follows

$$Y_t = A_t + TY_t + \Delta R_t - G_t + GBS_t - LR_t \qquad (6.2)$$

where $A$ is the value of domestic absorption, $P$ is the price level; $Y$ is the national income, $IR$ is the market interest rates, $EXR$ is the exchange rate, $TY$ is the government tax revenue, $G$ is the public consumption, $GBS$ is the government bond sales, $LR$ is the net lending by the central government to the states (which is not part of the planned public expenditure) and $\Delta R$ is the changes in the foreign exchange reserve reflecting the behaviour of the foreign trade sector.

The government budget deficit $(BD_t)$ is defined by equation (6.3)

$$BD_t = (G_t + LR_t + PF_t) - (TY_t + GBS_t + AF_t + BF_t) \qquad (6.3)$$

where $PF$ is the foreign payments due to existing foreign debts, which may include both amortization and interest payments, $AF$ is the foreign assistance which is an insignificant feature, $FB$ is the total foreign borrowing assuming only the government can borrow from foreign sources.

We assume $AF$ and $LR$ as exogenous, whereas $FB$, $G$ and $TY$ as policy instruments. $PF$ depends on the level of existing foreign debt and the world interest rate, although a sizable part of the foreign borrowing can be at a concessional rate

$$PF_t = a_4 + a_5 \sum_{\tau = -20}^{t} FB_\tau + a_6(WIR/EXR)_t \qquad (6.4)$$

Government bond sales (GBS) depends on its attractiveness reflected on the interest rate $(IR)$, on the ability of the domestic economy to absorb $(A)$, on the requirements of the governments $(G)$ and on the alternative sources of finances reflected on the tax revenue (TY) and on government's borrowing from the central bank i.e. NDA, the net domestic asset creation by the central bank.

$$GBS_t = a_7 + a_8 A_t + a_9 IR_t + a_{10} G_t - a_{11} TY_t - a_{12} NDA_t \qquad (6.5)$$

*Monetary sector*

We assume flow equilibrium in the money market, i.e.

$$\Delta MD = \Delta M = \Delta MS \tag{6.6}$$

where $MD$ is the money demand, $MS$ is the money supply. The stock of money supply depends on the stock of high powered money and the money-multiplier, as follows

$$MS_t = [(1 + CD)/(CD + RR)]_t \; (\Delta R + NDA)_t \tag{6.7}$$

$(\Delta R + NDA)$ reflect the stock of high powered money and the expression within the square bracket is the money multiplier which depends on credit to deposit ratio of the commercial banking sector ($CD$) and the reserve to deposit liabilities in the commercial banking sector ($RR$). Whereas $NDA$ is a instrument $\Delta R$ depends on the foreign trade sector. However the government can influence $CD$ and $RR$ to control the money supply. $RR$ which is the actual reserve ratio depends on the demand for loans created by private sectors and the commercial bank's willingness to lend. Actual reserve can be influenced by the statutory reserve limit set by the central bank; as in the case of India, the actual reserve is always at a higher level than the statutory reserve limit, so we accept, the reserve ratio for a developing country is mainly influenced by demand factors such as the market rate of interest and national income. If we assume that the desired reserve ratio $RR_t *$ is a function of national income and market interest rate i.e.

$$RR_t * = a_{13} + a_{14} Y + a_{15} \; IR_t \tag{6.8}$$

and the commercial banks may adjust their actual reserve ratio to the desired reserve ratio with a lag.

$$\Delta RR_t = \alpha(RR *_t - RR_{t-1}) \tag{6.9}$$

where $0 < \alpha < 1$; we can rewrite (6.8) as follows

$$RR_t = \alpha a_{13} + \alpha a_{14} \; Y + \alpha a_{15} \; IR_t + (1 - \alpha)RR_{t-1} \tag{6.10}$$

The ratio of currency to deposit liabilities with the commercial bank system is affected by the opportunity cost of holding currency as measured by the market interest rate and national income representing the domestic economic activity. Khan (1976) has postulated that the effect of national income should be negative because 'individuals and corporations tend to become more efficient in their management of cash balances as their income rises'. However a different logic may emerge to a developing country where the use of banks as institution is not widespread, particularly among the labour force, thus if there were an expansion in economic activity the entrepreneurs would have to maintain a huge cash-balance and run down deposits simply to pay various dues, because most payments would have to be made in cash. It is possible that corporations would be more efficient, with an initial adjustment lag. We therefore expect the sign of the coefficient for the current national income to be positive and that for the lagged national income to be negative.

$$CD_t = a_{16} + a_{17}\ IR_t + a_{18}\ Y_t - a_{19}\ Y_{t-1} \qquad (6.11)$$

The demand for money is assumed to be a function of the market interest rate and the national income.

$$(MD)_t = a_{20} - a_{21}\ (IR_t) + a_{22}\ (Yt) \qquad (6.12)$$

*Prices and interest rate*

The market rate of interest ($IR$) is determined by the supply of money, national income and the central bank discount rate.

$$IR_t = a_{23} - a_{29}(MS_t) + a_{29}\ (Y_t) + a_{26}(CI_t) \qquad (6.13)$$

The domestic price level depends on domestic economic activity, (particularly changes in the agricultural sector) and the import cost ($IMC$). The import cost in turn depends on the exchange rate ($EXR$) and world price of imported goods ($WPM$). We assume the desired price level ($P^*$) is represented by the following equation:

$$P^*_t = a_{27} - a_{28}\ (A_t) + a_{29}(IMC_t)$$

The desired price level reflects private sector's reaction to their expected domestic absorption of the expected import cost. Suppose the actual price will move according to the difference between the desired price in period $t$ and the actual price level in the previous period

$$\Delta P_t = \beta(P^*_t - P_{t-1});\ 0 < \beta < 1 \qquad (6.14)$$

Thus we get

$$P_t = \beta a_{27} - \beta a_{28}(A_t) + \beta a_{29}(IMC_t) + (1 - \beta)P_{t-1} \qquad (6.15)$$

import cost ($IMC$) is represented by the following equation

$$IMC_t = a_{30} + a_{31}(EXR_t) + a_{32}(WPM_t) \qquad (6.16)$$

The exchange rate $EXR$ can be an instrument variable whereas world prices of imported goods ($WPM$) is an exogenous variable.

*Balance of payments*

The balance of payments ($\Delta R$) is equal to the changes in the stock of international reserve i.e.

$$\Delta R_t = - M_t + \Delta K_t + PFT_t + FB_t - PF_t + AF_t \qquad (6.17)$$

when $X_t$ is the value of exports, $M_t$ is the value of imports, $\Delta K$ is the foreign capital inflows, $PFT$ is the private sectors transitions, $FB$ is the foreign borrowing, $PF$ is the foreign payments by the central bank and $AF$ is the foreign aid and grants; where $X_t$, $PFT_t$, $K_t$ and $AF_t$ are exogenous, import $M_t$ is determined by the national income, and the import cost i.e.

$$M_t = a_{33} + a_{34} Y_t - a_{35} (IMC_t) \qquad (6.18)$$

The above analytical structure was estimated using expected values of each variables, with expectations being adaptive. The estimated parameters were used as the initial starting point for the stochastic control model developed in the later chapters.

# 4 Estimation and analysis of the model

The analytical structure developed in Chapter 3 can be rewritten in the following expanded form, suitable for estimation (where E is the expectation operator).

$$E(A_t) = a_0 + a_1 E(Y)_t - a_2 E(IR)_t - a_3 E(EXR)_t + u_{1t} \qquad 1$$

$$Y_t = A_t + TY_t + \Delta R_t - G_t + GBS_t - LR_t \qquad 2$$

$$BD_t = (G_t + LR_t + PF_t) - (TY_t + GBS_t + AF_t + FB_t) \qquad 3$$

$$E(PF)_t = a_4 + a_5 - \sum_{\tau=-20}^{t} FB_\tau + R_6 E(WIR/EXR)_t + u_{2t} ; \qquad 4$$

$$E(GBS)_t = a_7 + a_8 E(A)_t + a_9 E(IR)_t + a_{10} E(G)_t - a_{11}$$
$$E(TY)_t - a_{12} E(NDA)_t + u_{3t} \qquad 5$$

$$MD = MS \qquad 6$$

$$E(MS)_t = \{(1 + E(CD))/(E(CD)_t + E(RR)_t)\} \cdot (R_t + NDA_t) \qquad 7$$

$$E(RR)_t = \alpha a_{13} + \alpha a_{14} E(Y)_t + \alpha a_{15} E(IR)_t + (1 - \alpha)$$
$$E(RR)_{t-1} + u_{4t} ; \; 0 < \alpha < 1; \qquad 8$$

$$E(CD)_t = a_{16} + a_{17} E(IR)_t + a_{18} E(Y)_t - a_{19} E(Y_{t-1}) + u_{5t} \qquad 9$$

$$E(MD)_t = a_{20} - a_{21} E(IR)_t + a_{22} E(Y_t) + u_{6t} \qquad 10$$

$$E(IR)_t = a_{23} E(MS)_t + a_{25} E(Y_t) + a_{26} (CI)_t + u_{7t} \qquad 11$$

$$E(P_t) = \beta a_{27} - \beta a_{28} E(A)_t + \beta a_{29} E(IMC)_t + (1 - \beta)$$
$$E(P)_{t-1} + u_{8t}; \; 0 < \beta < 1 \qquad 12$$

$$E(IMC)_t = a_{30} + a_{31}(EXR)_t + a_{32}(WPM)_t + u_{9t} \qquad 13$$

$$\Delta R_t = X_t - IM_t + K_t + PFT_t + FB_t - PF_t + AF_t \qquad 14$$

$$E(IM)_t = a_{33} + a_{34} E(Y)_t - a_{35} E(IMC)_t + u_{10t} \qquad 15$$

[where $0 < \alpha < 1$; $0 < \beta < 1$; $u_{it} \sim N(0, \sigma_i^2)$]

**Notations**

Notations are as follows:
- $A$ = Domestic Absorption
- $Y$ = GDP
- $IR$ = Interest rate in India (money market rate)
- $EXR$ = Exchange rate ( Rs/Us $)
- $TY$ = Government Tax Revenue
- $R$ = Foreign exchange reserve
- $\Delta R$ = Change in foreign exchange reserve
- $G$ = Government expenditure
- $GBS$ = Government bond sales
- $LR$ = Lending (minus repayments) to in. states
- $BD$ = Government budget deficit
- $PF$ = Foreign payments
- $AF$ = Foreign receipts (aid, grants, etc.)
- $FB$ = Foreign borrowing
- $WIR$ = World interest rate, average of European and US money market rate
- $NDA$ = Net domestic asset creation by the Reserve Bank of India
- $MD$ = Money demand
- $MS$ = Money supply
- $IM$ = value of import
- $CD$ = currency to deposit ratio of the commercial banking sector
- $RR$ = Reserve to deposit ratio of the commercial banking sector
- $CI$ = discount rate of the Reserve Bank of India
- $P$ = Consumer price index
- $X$ = value of Export
- $IMC$ = Import price index
- $K$ = Foreign capital inflows
- $PFT$ = Foreign private transaction
- $CFB$ = Cummulative foreign borrowing, i.e. foreign debt over a period of 20 years

Please note that $t$ indicates current time period, $t - 1$ indicates one year lag, $\Delta$ indicates changes. Sources of data International Financial Statistics of the I.M.F., Reserve Bank of India and Survey of Current Business.

In the above model we have 11 pure endegenous variables ($A, P, PF, GBS, MS, RR, CD, MD, IR, IMC$ and $IM$) and 12 pure endogenous variables ($EXR, TY, G, LR, AF, FB, WIR, NDA, CI, WPM, K, PFT$) apart from lagged exogenous variables. However, the estimated econometric model will have appropriate lag structure; thus it will create further lagged exogenous variables. The functional representations also may change reflecting problems in estimates.

## Estimations

The above model was estimated using annual data for the period of 1951 to 1985. Estimations were carried out in a number of different phases. First, the model was estimated by 2SLS using autoregressive error process to explore appropriate lag structure. These estimated parameters were used as initial guess for the FIML estimates of the model. The FIML estimates are as follows ($R^2$ and $\bar{R}^2$ refers to the corresponding 2SLS estimates).

## Estimated model

1. $A_t = 0.842Y_t + 0.024A_{t-1} - 1.319IR_t + 1.051IR_{t-1} - 2.84EXR_t + 55191.5$
   (3.48)   (1.74)   (1.34)   (1.16)   (1.29)   (4.87)
   $R^2 = 0.99, \bar{R}^2 = 0.92, DW = 1.76, \rho = 0.27$
   (1.31)

2. $(Y)_t = A_t + TY_t + \Delta R_t - G_t + GBS_t - LR_t$

3. $(BD)_t = (G_t + LR_t + PF_t) - (TY_t + GBS_t + AF_t + FB_t)$

4. $PF_t = 1148.80 + .169CFB_{t-1} + 144.374WIR_t$
   (1.48)   (2.39)   (1.89)
   $R^2 = .98, \bar{R}^2 = .92, DW = 2.07, \rho = 0.41$
   (1.71)

5. $GBS_t = 0.641G_t + 0.677G_{t-1} + 1.591IR_t - 0.33AF_t$
   (1.14)   (1.41)   (1.64)   (0.23)
   $R^2 = 0.89, \bar{R}^2 = 0.74, DW = 2.36, \rho = 0.23$
   (1.51)

6. $MD = MS$
7. $(MS)_t = \{(1+(CD)_t/(CD_t + RR_t)\}(R_t + NDA_t)$

8.  $RR_t = 0.008Y_t - 0.002Y_{t-1} + 1.2571R_t + 2.7031R_{t-1} - 0.003T + 0.065$
    (3.47)  (-1.84)  (1.87)  (1.88)  (2.87)  (2.72)
    $R^2 = 0.86, \bar{R}^2 = 0.79, DW = 2.88, \rho = 0.26$
    (1.23)

9.  $CD_t = -0.439IR_t + 0.158CD_{t-1} + 0.007Y_t + 0.009Y_{t-1} - 0.005T + 0.193$
    (-1.49)  (1.16)  (1.56)  (1.73)  (-6.269)  (11.95)
    $R^2 = 0.94, \bar{R}^2 = 0.92, DW = 1.22, \rho = 0.64$
    (4.21)

10. $MD_t = 2.733RR_t - 2.197IR_t + 1.713IR_{t-1} + 1.275Y_t - 113335.0$
    (-2.52)  (-0.24)  (2.17)  (6.67)  (-.088)
    $R^2 = .86, \bar{R}^2 = 0.81, DW = 1.92, \rho = 0.26$
    (1.31)

11. $IR_t = 0.413MD_{t-1} - 1.814IR_{t-1} + 8.656CI_t - 1.351CI_{t-1}$
    (1.93)  (1.403)  (1.68)  (-2.13)
    $+ 0.406Y_{t-1} - 7.02$
    (1.56)  (-1.84)
    $R^2 = 0.98, \bar{R}^2 = 0.98, DW = 2.09, \rho = .58$
    (3.21)

12. $P_t = -0.0004A_t + 0.0002A_t + 0.105IMC_t + 0.421P_{t-1} + 32.895$
    (-5.71)  (1.77)  (1.48)  (3.79)  (1.87)
    $R^2 = 0.98, \bar{R}^2 = 0.93, DW = 2.09, \rho = 0.58$

13. $IMC_t = 5.347 + 19.352WPM_t + 9.017EXR_t$
    (1.34)  (2.03)  (0.97)
    $R^2 = .98, \bar{R}^2 = .97, DW = 2.07, \rho = .31$
    (1.37)

14. $\Delta R_t = X_t - IM_t + K_t + PFT_t + FB_t - PF_t + AF_t$

15. $IM_t = -24.04 - 0.025IM_{t-1} + 0.104Y_t - 0.089Y_{t-1} - 0.654IMC_t + 1.123T$
    (-0.82)  (-0.86)  (1.59)  (9.21)  (-1.26)  (0.27)
    $R^2 = 0.96, \bar{R}^2 = 0.92, DW = 2.52, \rho = -0.62$
    (-1.72)

16. $CFB_t = \sum_{r=-20}^{t} FB_r$
    $\lambda^2 = 563.09.$

## Explanation of the equation structure

The initial estimates presented above indicate the system which will serve as the initial starting point of the iterative process of the adaptive control system. The equations are estimated first by 2SLS and using those estimates we have obtained FIML estimates.

Equation 1 indicates absorption is negatively related to both current interest rate and the exchange rate. However, the net steady state effect of the interest rate is low, indicating the fact that the interest rate can have less influence on absorption than that expected in a fully monetized economy. At the same time, exchange rate devaluation can affect absorption negatively, thereby indicating the strong influence of the foreign trade sector on the domestic economy, which is somehow unexpected given the small contribution foreign trade sectors have on the gross national income.

Equation 4 indicates the foreign payments, $PF$ (includes both amortization on existing principal foreign debt and interest payments) is influenced by the existing foreign debt, $CFB$ (cummulated over the last twenty years) and world interest rate $WIR$ which is the weighted average of the US and the European interest rate.

Equation 5 indicates that government bond sales, $GBS_t$ are significantly related to the public expenditure, interest rate and foreign receipts. Other variables (absorption, tax rate and money supply) mentioned in the analytical structure of the model are not significant determinant of the government bond sales. Although it is not expected that planned absorption and tax revenue should affect bond sales, however, in India bond sale is accepted as a normal means of generating public revenues rather than an instrument of last resort. Part of the explanation is the unpopularity of increased tax rates and less than expected return from tax efforts. Because public expenditure can affect domestic absorption directly, bond sale is influenced quite significantly.

Equation 8 indicates that the actual reserve ratio is determined positively by the steady state $Y$, and also the rate of interest. The actual reserve ratio in India is more than the statutory reserve ratio set by the Reserve Bank of India, so factors affecting demand for credit determine the actual reserve ratio. Because the role of the public sector is so prominent, increased national income means increased public expenditure, which pushes up government bond sales, that can reduce deposit within the commercial banking system. This phenomenon can explain the positive relationship between reserve to deposit ratio and the steady state national income.

Similarly Equation (9) indicates the influence of demand for bank credit in terms of currency to deposit ratio, $CD$ is positively influenced by $Y$ and negatively by the steady state rate of interest. The negative influence $T$ in both Equations (8) and (9) indicates increasing demand for credit in the economy as a result of increased economic activity and the willingness of the commercial banking system to extend credit to the private sector.

Equation (10) is the money demand equation where, apart from the national income and interest rate, reserve ratio can play an important part. If a commercial banking system is unwilling to expand credit, deposit creation will be slowed down, reserve ratio will go up and money demand will go down. In an economy like India, where banks are under public control, it is realistic to accept this role of the commercial banking system in the money-demand function.

Equation (11) implies that the market rate of interest is most strongly influenced by the central bank's discount rate incorporating both $Y$ and $MD$ indicating that if $Y$ goes up, public expenditure needs to go up and, as a result, the Government's bond sales will go up, which will push up the market interest rate. However, MD indicates mainly private sector's demand for money.

The interaction of private, public and the foreign trade sector is most prominent in the equation for price determination. Equation (12) indicates that the general price index depends on the steady state domestic absorption negatively, which implies the effects of the domestic supplies on prices. At the same time import cost ($IMC$) affects $P$ quite significantly. For equation (13), $IMC$ depends on the exchange rate and the world price of importables. Equation (15) determines imports in terms of national income and import cost. The positive effect of the time trend variable indicates gradual relaxation of input control measures.

## Dynamic properties of the model

There are three questions we can ask:
(a) whether the model is stable;
(b) how sensitive the endogenous variables of the models are to the changes in the exogenous variables (i.e. the nature of the response multiplier);
(c) how the response multiplier will change over time under adaptive control systems.

For (a) we have derived the real characteristic roots of the system and tested the hypothesis that they are within the unit circle (Box and Pearce, 1970). The roots are as follows:

## Table 4.1
### Real characteristic roots of the model
real roots

-0.0000008
-0.0000008
-0.1213610
0.2442519
0.3087129
0.5123629
0.7834260
0.0000001
0.0000001

All the real roots are less than unity, so the system is stable. [In the equivalent control system, the rank of the controllability matrix is the same as the dimension of the reduced state vector so that the system to controllable and observable, i.e. system parameters can be identified.]

We can, however, transform our model to the following form:

$$Y_t = \rho Y_{t-1} + e_t, \quad t = 1, 2, \ldots,$$

where $\rho$ is a real number and $\{e_t\}$ is a sequence of normally distributed random variables with mean zero and variance $\sigma^2$. Box and Pearce (1970) had suggested the following test statistic:

$$Q_K = n \sum_{k=1}^{K} r_k^2,$$

$n$ = the number of observations where

$$\text{where} \quad r_K = \left(\sum_{t=1}^{n} \hat{e}_t^2\right)^{-1} \sum_{t=k+1}^{n} \hat{e}_t \hat{e}_{t-k},$$

and $\hat{e}_t$ are the residuals from the fitted model.

If $\{Y_t\}$ satisfies the system then, under the null hypothesis, $Q_K$ is distributed as a chi-squared random variable with $K - P$ degrees of freedom where $P$ is the number of parameters estimated. The null hypothesis is that $\rho = 1$ where $e_t = Y_t - Y_{t-1}$ and thus $P = 0$. The estimated $Q_K$ is 3.85 where the null hypothesis is rejected at the 5 per cent confidence. So we accept the alternative hypothesis that if $\rho < 1$, then the system is stable.

## Response multiplier

In our adaptive control model, the response multiplier will move from one period to another. A part of the response multiplier for the initial period of planning is as follows.

## Table 4.2
### Response multiplier* and endogenous variable

| Exogenous Variable | Y | GBS | P | BD | CD | MS | IR |
|---|---|---|---|---|---|---|---|
| EXR | -.02283 | -.00027 | .05593 | .00121 | -.00018 | -.00576 | -.00004 |
| G | .03178 | .00095 | .13965 | .04073 | .00041 | .01699 | .00108 |
| TY | -.03116 | -.00426 | -.15022 | .04091 | -.00310 | -.03637 | -.01231 |
| CI | -.00265 | .04953 | -.00884 | .00550 | -.00210 | -.00625 | .06599 |

*Note: This response multiplier refers to the initial period only.

As it is obvious from the response multiplier devaluation will have a negative effect on national income, it will also have negative effects on government bond sales, currency to deposit ratio, interest rate and on the money demand. It is due to the fact that Indian exports are not elastic in response to devaluation whereas devaluation will reduce import abilities significantly. As a result, national income and domestic activity will have negative effects which will depress the private sector. As a result CD will go down. Due to the down-turn of the economic activity, there will be less demand for loans, so market interest rate will go down and there will be less demand for government bonds. Devaluations also can have inflationary effect due to increased import costs.

Government expenditure on the other hand will have positive effects on every variable, which implies increased public expenditure and will stimulate the national income and the private sector as well, despite increased interest rates. However, it will have inflationary impact at the same time.

Increased tax revenues will depress the national income, as it will reduce government bond sales. Lower level of national income will reduce money supply, and the private sector's activity which will be reflected in the reduced currency to deposit ratio, and the reduced level of money demand (and money supply). Reduced level of national income in this case will have reduced price level and, at the same time, private sector activity will be reduced (as reflected in the currency to deposit ratio and money demand) due to increased market rate of interest. Although government bond sales will go up, budget deficit will be increased due to reduced level of economic activity.

## Dynamics of response multipliers

The response multipliers of the system will move over time within an adaptive control framework. The movement of the response multiplier should be slow (see Tsakalis and Ioannou, 1990; Das and Cristi, 1990).

## Table 4.3
### Response multiplier – period 1*

| Endogenous | Y | GBS | P | BD | CD | MS | IR |
|---|---|---|---|---|---|---|---|
| EXR | -0.2254 | -.00092 | .05458 | .00111 | -.00020 | -.00543 | -.00092 |
| G | .03572 | .00403 | .14849 | .03987 | .00500 | .01466 | .00330 |
| TY | -.03590 | -.01017 | -.15549 | .02791 | -.00399 | -.02682 | -.01996 |
| CI | -.00226 | .04592 | -.00606 | .00458 | -.00169 | -.00516 | .06120 |

* Note: Period 2 refers to the first period of the planning horizon.

### Response multiplier – period 2

| Endogenous | Y | GBS | P | BD | CD | MS | IR |
|---|---|---|---|---|---|---|---|
| EXR | -.02209 | -.00096 | .05336 | .00125 | -.00013 | -.00570 | -.00097 |
| G | .03293 | .00568 | .15603 | .03500 | .00091 | .02882 | .00599 |
| TY | -.02961 | -.01240 | -.15688 | .02792 | -.00246 | -.04758 | -.02324 |
| CI | -.00273 | .94546 | -.00387 | .00488 | -.00181 | -.00668 | .06057 |

### Response multiplier – period 3

| Endogenous | Y | GBS | P | BD | CD | MS | IR |
|---|---|---|---|---|---|---|---|
| EXR | -.02199 | -.00069 | .05269 | .00133 | -.00042 | -.00573 | -.00062 |
| G | .03001 | .00499 | .16536 | .02924 | .05923 | .04217 | .00570 |
| TY | -.02470 | -.01149 | -.16281 | .02472 | -.07031 | -.06325 | -.02220 |
| CI | -.00215 | .04676 | -.00252 | .00399 | -.00465 | -.00671 | .06228 |

## Response multiplier – period 5

| Endogenous | Y | GBS | P | BD | CD | MS | IR |
|---|---|---|---|---|---|---|---|
| EXR | -.02133 | -.00088 | .05190 | .00152 | -.00201 | -.00595 | -.00089 |
| G | .02058 | .00558 | .18078 | .01160 | .50890 | .07248 | .00530 |
| TY | -.01676 | -.00410 | -.16655 | .00695 | -.55026 | -.07779 | -.01013 |
| CI | -.00268 | .04465 | -.00267 | .00403 | -.01967 | -.00726 | .05953 |

## Response multiplier – period 7

| Endogenous | Y | GBS | P | BD | CD | MS | IR |
|---|---|---|---|---|---|---|---|
| EXR | -.02067 | -.00116 | .04987 | .00135 | -.00104 | -.00558 | -.00129 |
| G | .00733 | .01033 | .16455 | .00048 | .57357 | .10760 | .01206 |
| TY | -.00402 | -.00345 | -.14832 | .01434 | -.58067 | -.10904 | -.00869 |
| CI | -.00200 | .04174 | -.00236 | .00293 | -.02186 | -.00551 | .05566 |

As we can see from the above, the coefficients may go up or down and the degree of variation differs from one period to another which are related to the movements of the policy variables for those periods.

## Table 4.4
## Monetary dynamics

| | \multicolumn{5}{c}{periods} | | | | |
|---|---|---|---|---|---|
| | 1 | 2 | 3 | 5 | 7 |
| $\dfrac{dMS}{dCI}$ | -.00516 | -.00668 | -.00671 | -.00726 | -.00551 |
| $\dfrac{dIR}{dCI}$ | .06120 | .06057 | .06228 | .05953 | .05566 |
| $\dfrac{dP}{dCI}$ | -.00606 | -.00387 | -.00252 | -.00267 | -.00236 |
| $\dfrac{dMS}{dEXR}$ | -.00543 | -.00570 | -.00573 | -.00595 | -.00558 |
| $\dfrac{dIR}{dEXR}$ | -.00092 | -.00097 | -.00062 | -.00089 | -.00129 |
| $\dfrac{dP}{dEXR}$ | .04548 | .05336 | .05269 | .05190 | .04987 |

## Fiscal dynamics

| | \multicolumn{5}{c}{periods} | | | | |
|---|---|---|---|---|---|
| | 1 | 2 | 3 | 5 | 7 |
| $\dfrac{dP}{dG}$ | .14849 | .15603 | .16536 | .18078 | .16455 |
| $\dfrac{dY}{dG}$ | .03572 | .03203 | .03001 | .02058 | .00733 |
| $\dfrac{dP}{dTY}$ | -.15549 | -.15688 | -.16281 | -.16655 | -.14832 |
| $\dfrac{dY}{dTY}$ | -.03590 | -.02691 | -.02470 | -.01676 | -.00402 |
| $\dfrac{dGBS}{dG}$ | .00403 | .00568 | .00499 | .00558 | .01033 |

## Monetary dynamics

The exchange rate can afford prices in a significant way, although in effect prices decline slightly on the planning period. The exchange rate can afford interest rate slightly, i.e. devaluation will induce lower interest rate, mainly due to the fact that devaluation will increase prices, as a result interest rates will have to be reduced in order to reduce the cost of borrowing and as a result cost of production, otherwise there will be inflectionary spirals. However the impact of the exchange rate on the interest rate is very insignificant and will go up slightly over the planning period. The exchange rate devaluation will lead to reductions in money supply. The devaluation will induce inflection, so as to combat further inflection money supply it will then go down. The impact of the exchange rate on money supply will increase over the planning period, although in the last year it will decline mainly due to the fact at the same year the impact of the exchange rate on prices will be reduced.

## Fiscal dynamics

We can analyze the impact of the public expenditure and tax revenues on the two most important variables, GNP ($Y$) and price level ($P$). The government expenditure ($G$) will certainly increase price level and the impact will be intensified. The impact of the government expenditure on the GNP will be reduced gradually, it is consistent with the reduced impacts of the tax revenues on the GNP over the planning period. Tax revenue will have negative impacts on the GNP and the impacts will decline over time. Tax revenue will have negative impacts on price level as well. The negative impacts of the tax revenue on the GNP is partly explained by the negative impact of tax revenue on the currency to deposit ratios of the commercial banks, the main indicator for rate sector activities.

The government expenditure also have positive impacts on the governments bond sales and that impact will increase over time due to the increasing difficulties of raising taxes which will have negative impacts on the growth prospects.

However, it is not possible to analyze full impacts of monetary and fixed policies without analyzing their optimum paths over the planning horizon. The following chapter is intended for that purpose.

# 5 Analysis of the result of the control system

In this Chapter, a complete analysis of the results obtained using adaptive control system are described with two separate purposes. The first purpose of the analysis is to compare the optimal solutions with the historical data over an experimental period between 1978 to 1986. In this analysis, three different types of control solutions are compared.

The second purpose of the analysis is to present a formal planned solution of the economy in terms of adaptive control with two alternative objectives: growth and price stability. Analysis of the results obtained in each of the regimes, i.e. regime with emphasis on growth and regime with emphasis on price stability, are then compared. However, it is essential to point out the model and the planned solution presents an idea of planning that does not exist in India. The idea is to replace physical controls over the private sectors by monetary and financial controls. In this model attempts are made to represent monetary and financial controls in terms of various commercial banking instruments, control banking instruments and various financial instruments in the hands of the central government. Liberalization of this type can certainly create an enthusiasm which cannot be quantified. So our results are at best an underestimation of what might have happened if a government would replace physical controls by financial and monetary controls.

## Table 5.1
### Historical path: 1978 - 1986
### (in 1979 price - billion Rs)

|      | (X-M)+FPT | A        | Y        | G      | NMS    | NDA    |
|------|-----------|----------|----------|--------|--------|--------|
| 1978 | -7.868    | 762.707  | 946.87   | 205.53 | 204.75 | 121.78 |
| 1979 | -25.056   | 921.346  | 1044.62  | 224.22 | 277.67 | 144.05 |
| 1980 | -26.132   | 936.005  | 1080.00  | 213.23 | 324.60 | 163.12 |
| 1981 | -16.039   | 959.721  | 1104.85  | 265.94 | 368.74 | 190.58 |
| 1982 | -9.665    | 989.009  | 1154.05  | 235.84 | 362.94 | 195.02 |
| 1983 | -11.624   | 1002.929 | 1173.52  | 297.52 | 402.17 | 225.81 |
| 1984 | -21.468   | 949.774  | 1262.52  | 350.02 | 451.73 | 251.10 |
| 1985 | -23.673   | 959.615  | 1308.50  | 392.11 | 485.39 | 271.50 |
| 1986 | -19.995   | 1002.021 | 1357.57  | 396.52 | 563.46 | 290.14 |

|      | RR   | CD  | IR (%) | CI (%) | IMC (1978=100) | EXR (Rs/US $) | CCR  |
|------|------|-----|--------|--------|----------------|---------------|------|
| 1978 | .127 | .79 | 8.47   | 9.0    | 100            | 8.12          | .11  |
| 1979 | .126 | .79 | 7.24   | 9.0    | 116            | 7.86          | .13  |
| 1980 | .120 | .81 | 8.61   | 10.0   | 110            | 8.66          | .13  |
| 1981 | .130 | .81 | 7.27   | 10.0   | 113            | 9.45          | .12  |
| 1982 | .121 | .81 | 8.30   | 10.0   | 115            | 10.45         | .13  |
| 1983 | .110 | .82 | 9.95   | 10.0   | 117            | 11.36         | .12  |
| 1984 | .149 | .79 | 10.0   | 10.0   | 119            | 12.37         | .11  |
| 1985 | .155 | .77 | 9.97   | 10.0   | 121            | 12.61         | .15  |
| 1986 | .159 | .75 | 9.83   | 10.0   | 120            | 12.96         | .16  |

|      | GBS    | BD     | LR    | TY     | FB-FP | P(1978=100) |
|------|--------|--------|-------|--------|-------|-------------|
| 1978 | 56.24  | 59.04  | 48.53 | 134.06 | 4.72  | 100.0       |
| 1979 | 70.29  | 74.67  | 62.23 | 135.63 | 5.86  | 106.2       |
| 1980 | 54.70  | 65.04  | 58.58 | 145.24 | 6.83  | 118.4       |
| 1981 | 91.84  | 74.12  | 63.62 | 155.37 | 8.23  | 133.8       |
| 1982 | 52.79  | 82.27  | 64.52 | 157.37 | 7.93  | 144.4       |
| 1983 | 92.08  | 100.24 | 71.46 | 168.78 | 7.88  | 161.5       |
| 1984 | 112.77 | 120.17 | 85.25 | 194.94 | 7.39  | 175.0       |
| 1985 | 129.29 | 133.27 | 90.15 | 210.00 | 9.70  | 184.7       |
| 1986 | 114.22 | 119.74 | 71.51 | 222.41 | 11.60 | 200.8       |

## Table 5.2
### Target paths
### (in 1978 price - billion Rs)

|      | (X-M+FPT) | A    | Y      | G      | NMS   | NDA   |
|------|-----------|------|--------|--------|-------|-------|
| 1978 | -1.8      | 720  | 963.0  | 185.33 | 142.0 | 140.0 |
| 1979 | -2.5      | 740  | 1040.5 | 215.56 | 158.0 | 150.0 |
| 1980 | -2.7      | 770  | 1128.9 | 269.43 | 160.0 | 155.0 |
| 1981 | -2.8      | 820  | 1219.2 | 248.29 | 162.0 | 158.0 |
| 1982 | -2.8      | 860  | 1316.7 | 321.11 | 164.0 | 160.0 |
| 1983 | -2.8      | 920  | 1422.1 | 370.83 | 166.0 | 162.0 |
| 1984 | -2.9      | 980  | 1535.9 | 422.81 | 167.0 | 162.0 |
| 1985 | -2.9      | 1050 | 1658.8 | 448.67 | 169.0 | 165.0 |
| 1986 | -2.9      | 1190 | 1700.0 | 439.67 | 171.0 | 167.0 |

|      | RR | CD  | IR (%) | CI (%) | EXR (Rs/US$) | CCR | P (1978=100) |
|------|----|----|--------|--------|--------------|-----|--------------|
| 1978 | .1 | .7  | 8.05 | 9.0 | 8.18 | .11 | 100 |
| 1979 | .1 | .65 | 8.0  | 8.0 | 8.0  | .11 | 105 |
| 1980 | .1 | .65 | 8.0  | 7.0 | 8.0  | .11 | 110 |
| 1981 | .1 | .65 | 8.0  | 6.6 | 8.0  | .11 | 117 |
| 1982 | .1 | .65 | 8.0  | 6.0 | 8.0  | .11 | 122 |
| 1983 | .1 | .65 | 7.5  | 6.0 | 8.0  | .11 | 128 |
| 1984 | .1 | .65 | 7.0  | 6.0 | 8.0  | .11 | 135 |
| 1985 | .1 | .65 | 6.5  | 6.0 | 8.0  | .11 | 145 |
| 1986 | .1 | .65 | 6.5  | 6.0 | 8.0  | .11 | 155 |

|      | GBS    | BD     | LR   | TY    | FB-FP |
|------|--------|--------|------|-------|-------|
| 1978 | 31.50  | 73.23  | 22.1 | 97.0  | 5.7   |
| 1979 | 42.11  | 83.75  | 24.7 | 108.0 | 5.8   |
| 1980 | 57.26  | 113.27 | 27.7 | 120.6 | 6.0   |
| 1981 | 78.45  | 60.84  | 31.0 | 133.8 | 6.2   |
| 1982 | 108.26 | 91.95  | 34.1 | 148.6 | 6.4   |
| 1983 | 149.40 | 87.93  | 37.5 | 164.4 | 6.6   |
| 1984 | 206.17 | 68.04  | 41.2 | 183.1 | 6.7   |
| 1985 | 284.50 | 50.0   | 45.4 | 203.2 | 6.9   |
| 1986 | 300.0  | 117.9  | 49.0 | 220.0 | 7.0   |

## Table 5.3
### Optimal adaptive control paths
### (in 1978 price - billion Rs)

|      | (X-M+FPT) | A       | Y       | G      | NMS    | NDA    |
|------|-----------|---------|---------|--------|--------|--------|
| 1978 | -3.15     | 723.57  | 939.84  | 177.77 | 115.51 | 101.68 |
| 1979 | -3.5      | 749.33  | 1003.50 | 209.20 | 117.15 | 103.70 |
| 1980 | -3.9      | 772.95  | 1029.20 | 203.55 | 134.54 | 118.39 |
| 1981 | -11.9     | 829.69  | 1105.40 | 263.90 | 164.75 | 144.98 |
| 1982 | -15.8     | 859.79  | 1157.70 | 247.74 | 109.38 | 149.05 |
| 1983 | -17.8     | 916.46  | 1230.90 | 311.85 | 206.42 | 181.05 |
| 1984 | -15.9     | 975.49  | 1305.40 | 358.40 | 257.97 | 227.02 |
| 1985 | -18.9     | 1045.80 | 1398.90 | 409.89 | 295.84 | 266.34 |
| 1986 | -18.2     | 1139.80 | 1453.40 | 404.63 | 329.80 | 290.22 |

|      | RR   | CD  | IR (%) | CI (%) | EXR (Rs/US$) | CCR | P (1978=100) |
|------|------|-----|--------|--------|--------------|-----|--------------|
| 1978 | .103 | .83 | 5.73   | 8.06   | 7.23         | .11 | 107          |
| 1979 | .106 | .85 | 5.91   | 7.73   | 6.76         | .11 | 112          |
| 1980 | .106 | .82 | 5.37   | 6.44   | 6.30         | .10 | 110          |
| 1981 | .104 | .86 | 5.89   | 5.74   | 4.83         | .10 | 112          |
| 1982 | .103 | .83 | 5.85   | 6.37   | 7.87         | .10 | 118          |
| 1983 | .101 | .81 | 6.39   | 6.92   | 8.56         | .11 | 122          |
| 1984 | .101 | .86 | 6.16   | 6.70   | 9.04         | .11 | 138          |
| 1985 | .102 | .88 | 6.23   | 6.46   | 10.24        | .11 | 146          |
| 1986 | .103 | .87 | 6.94   | 6.78   | 13.12        | .11 | 158          |

|      | GBS    | BD     | LR     | TY     | FB-FP |
|------|--------|--------|--------|--------|-------|
| 1978 | 19.29  | 72.81  | 24.52  | 105.09 | 5.09  |
| 1979 | 18.99  | 89.37  | 28.47  | 123.60 | 5.71  |
| 1980 | 27.23  | 79.84  | 32.24  | 123.47 | 5.24  |
| 1981 | 36.82  | 125.16 | 37.9   | 134.30 | 5.52  |
| 1982 | 45.59  | 85.73  | 44.43  | 154.30 | 6.55  |
| 1983 | 61.87  | 139.05 | 61.79  | 164.76 | 7.96  |
| 1984 | 86.81  | 175.97 | 80.96  | 168.44 | 8.13  |
| 1985 | 103.51 | 216.99 | 103.15 | 184.04 | 8.49  |
| 1986 | 143.67 | 167.37 | 117.03 | 201.42 | 9.20  |

## Table 5.4
## Optimal stochastic control paths
## (in 1978 price - billion Rs)

|      | (X-M+FPT) | A       | Y       | G      | NMS    | NDA    |
|------|-----------|---------|---------|--------|--------|--------|
| 1978 | -3.17     | 715.2   | 901.49  | 159.94 | 114.27 | 100.54 |
| 1979 | -3.5      | 735.8   | 953.45  | 186.49 | 114.96 | 101.17 |
| 1980 | -3.7      | 755.62  | 970.48  | 178.06 | 131.57 | 115.78 |
| 1981 | -10.5     | 808.39  | 1037.5  | 231.82 | 160.57 | 141.31 |
| 1982 | -13.9     | 833.49  | 1072.3  | 210.29 | 164.25 | 144.55 |
| 1983 | -16.5     | 883.92  | 1131.4  | 265.41 | 198.99 | 175.11 |
| 1984 | -15.4     | 938.47  | 1198.7  | 307.35 | 248.18 | 218.41 |
| 1985 | -16.5     | 999.90  | 1270.8  | 345.69 | 282.82 | 248.88 |
| 1986 | -16.1     | 1108.30 | 1383.9  | 378.36 | 320.82 | 282.33 |

|      | RR   | CD  | IR (%) | CI (%) | EXR (Rs/US$) | CCR | P (1978=100) |
|------|------|-----|--------|--------|--------------|-----|--------------|
| 1978 | .103 | .76 | 6.91   | 8.61   | 7.44         | .12 | 108          |
| 1979 | .105 | .77 | 6.00   | 7.38   | 7.78         | .12 | 112          |
| 1980 | .104 | .82 | 5.45   | 6.12   | 7.62         | .13 | 110          |
| 1981 | .102 | .86 | 5.87   | 6.42   | 6.35         | .13 | 110          |
| 1982 | .102 | .89 | 5.54   | 6.87   | 9.64         | .12 | 121          |
| 1983 | .103 | .88 | 6.00   | 6.50   | 10.71        | .13 | 130          |
| 1984 | .101 | .74 | 6.55   | 6.50   | 11.47        | .12 | 146          |
| 1985 | .101 | .77 | 6.27   | 6.46   | 12.44        | .12 | 152          |
| 1986 | .103 | .76 | 6.32   | 6.25   | 16.27        | .13 | 165          |

|      | GBS    | BD     | LR     | TY     | FB-FP |
|------|--------|--------|--------|--------|-------|
| 1978 | 21.17  | 72.00  | 24.52  | 86.24  | 4.98  |
| 1979 | 21.69  | 86.58  | 28.47  | 100.96 | 5.71  |
| 1980 | 29.89  | 76.88  | 30.24  | 98.29  | 5.23  |
| 1981 | 38.03  | 118.34 | 37.90  | 107.95 | 5.39  |
| 1982 | 44.16  | 78.75  | 42.25  | 124.07 | 5.56  |
| 1983 | 59.81  | 126.05 | 58.85  | 132.07 | 6.32  |
| 1984 | 83.87  | 156.78 | 78.18  | 140.07 | 7.81  |
| 1985 | 98.42  | 181.18 | 97.87  | 156.19 | 7.76  |
| 1986 | 141.61 | 195.97 | 116.14 | 147.87 | 9.06  |

## Analysis over the history: 1977-1985

In this analysis, attempts were made to compare three different types of optimal solutions: deterministic, stochastic and adaptive. The first purpose here is to compare these solutions and to see how we gain from adaptive control solutions. The second purpose is to examine the efficiencies of the policies undertaken during that period. For that reason, the objective function is set up with the objectives similar to that of the Indian Planning Commission with similar target growth rates for major macro economic variables. The characteristics of the target paths along with historical paths and the optimal solutions are given in Table 5.1 to 5.4.

We analyze the results as follows:-

*a) National income and domestic absorption*

In the target path it is assumed the domestic absorption should be Rs 720 bill in 1978, which will reach Rs 860 bill in 1982 (at constant 1978 price) and will reach Rs 1190 bill in 1986. The historical path has not performed badly compared to the target path. In the historical path the corresponding figures are Rs 762.7 bill in 1978, Rs 989 bill in 1982 and Rs 1002 bill in 1986. That period has seen unprecedented growth in Indian exports to the Middle East and economic expansions due to a combination of factors like increased foreign exchange earnings, good agricultural seasons and liberalized economic policy initiated in 1984. The stochastic control path shows an improved performance with domestic absorption going up from Rs 715 bill in 1978 to Rs 833 bill in 1982 and Rs 1108 bill in 1986. The corresponding adaptive path demonstrates a better performance when the domestic absorption went up from Rs 723 bill in 1978 to Rs 859 bill in 1982 and to Rs 1139 bill in 1986. The improved performance of the adaptive control solutions were achieved with less tax burdens, but with slightly higher amount of net money creation (NDA). However, the significant features are the central banks discount rate (CI) and credit to deposit ratio (CD) of the commercial banks; both of these are significantly lower along the adaptive control path compared to their corresponding historical paths. As a result, market interest rates will be much lower along the adaptive path compared to those on the historical paths. However, the budget deficits along the adaptive and stochastic paths are much higher than that along the historical paths. As a result the requirements for public borrowings will be higher along the stochastic and adaptive paths.

*b) Prices*

Price indices along the historical path is much higher than those along either stochastic or adaptive control solution paths. Historical price index went up from 100 in 1978 to 151.9 in 1982 and to 204.6 in 1986. The corresponding figures in the adaptive solution are 107 in 1978, 118 in 1982 and 158 in 1986. The stochastic solution presents a similar picture. The explanation can be obtained in terms of higher rate of central bank discount rate and higher rate of interest in the historical period which was responsible for the higher cost of borrowing which must have pushed up prices, compared to that in the adaptive or stochastic solution. A slightly higher rate of devaluation of the Rupees along the historical path compared to either on the stochastic or adaptive path also may have contributed to the higher import costs over the historical period.

*c) Balance of payment*

Net deficit in trade (X-M +FPT) in the historical path went up from Rs 7.86 bill in 1978 to Rs 9.66 bill in 1982 and to Rs 19.99 bill in 1986. The corresponding figures in the adaptive path are Rs 3.1 bill in 1978, Rs 15.8 in 1982 and Rs 18.2 in 1986. The stochastic path is not very different from the adaptive path. Net deficit in trade over the historical path went up significantly from the year 1979 mainly due to India's increased foreign exchange reserve and due to increased import cost as a result of the increased price of crude petroleum and the increased need for defence related imports. In the control solution the growth of net trade deficit was gradual and the total volume of net deficit over the period between 1978 and 1986 is much less than that in the historical path. As a result the net foreign borrowings over the historical path are more than that along the stochastic path. Foreign borrowing historically has increased from Rs 4.7 bill in 1976 to Rs 11.6 bill in 1986, however the corresponding figures over the adaptive path were Rs 5.09 bill in 1978 and Rs 9.2 bill in 1986.

*d) Monetary policies*

Monetary instruments in this analysis can be separated into two different types; (a) banking instruments including central banking instruments and (b) partly market driven instruments such as interest rate and exchange rate. Among the former, we have NDA (net domestic asset creation by the central bank), RR (commercial banks reserve ratio), CD (credit to deposit ratios of the commercial banks) and CI (central banks discount rate) because the interest rate is mainly influenced by the central banks discount rate and the exchange rate is within the managed floating system in India, so they are only partly market driven. Newly created money stock (NHS) which is in our definition the money supply is the result of these policies. Money demand is influenced by the interest rate and national income and their expectations, which are influenced by the announced targets and private sectors expectations regarding their achievements. As a result, expectations of the public policy instruments like NDA and CI may not match that of the private sector as reflected through RR, CD, MD. (see Congdon, 1990 for similar analysis regarding monetary equilibrium). In our experiment, historical path demonstrates a higher magnitude for NMS and NDA compared to the stochastic and adaptive path. Similar features are noted for CI, and, as a result IR. Along the historical path CD is above CD the adaptive and stochastic path and RR is much less than RR the stochastic or adaptive path. If we try to analyze their impacts on the policies, we can see influences of the historical policies. Price indices along the historical path above price indices along the stochastic or adaptive paths. It may imply that lower interest rate as suggested by the optimal control solutions does not necessarily mean higher rate of inflation if lower cost of borrowing can increase the real output of the economy at a faster rate than under a 'higher cost of borrowing' regime. However from this result we cannot necessarily draw the conclusion that the Indian monetary authority was wrong to follow a high interest rate. We consider IR as the interest rate; due to the absence of long enough historical time-series it was not possible to include lending rate in the model, but the lending rate is normally about 7 per cent higher than the money market rate). In the control experiment all exogenous variables are assumed to be the same as their historical values. It is not possible for any policy marker to know in advance the behaviour of the exogenous variables. As a result policies may overshoot, which is the possible case here. It was not correct to push up the cost of borrowing by increasing the rate of interest. The high growth economies like Germany and Japan can point out the similar direction where during the 1950s and 1960s interest rates were kept low and RR and CD's were kept high to stimulate the real economy. South Korea has followed similar policies.

*External sector*

In the external side, exchange rate policies over the historical period show when balance of payments were in high deficits from 1979 to 1981, there were not much devaluation, but it took place afterwards during the period 1983-1986. The deficits during the former period (in 1979-1981) were due to the increased cost of imports of crude petroleum. The deficits in the latter period were due to liberalization policies introduced since 1984-1985 as a result of which import went up at a significant rate. As far as the deficits were due to external factors these would be beyond the control of the planner but in the 'control' solution, deficits went up gradually rather than in a cyclical fashion thereby creating instability in the country's foreign exchange reserve. The foreign exchange rate in the control solutions were devalued gradually and at a faster rate at the end of the experimental period. Foreign borrowing went up significantly during the historical period; because the balance of payments deficits were due to either external factors or due to exogenous policy changes, volumes of foreign debt in the control solutions cannot be significantly reduced. However, because the volume of deficits of the balance were lower along the historical path, the net foreign borrowings along the control solutions are lower than those along the historical path. It was not the purpose of the control experiments to minimize foreign borrowing in those circumstances. The control solutions would produce different profiles for real outputs and for every other variables. Foreign borrowing was increasing at an alarming rate much due to some structural problems (i.e. slow growth of exports and increasing import demands) thus creating a serious obstacle for further growth prospects.

*Financial policies*

Financial policies in our model comprises public expenditures and grants to the states on the expenditure side and government bond sales and tax revenues on the income side. The budget deficit is the result of those. The public expenditures and lending to the states are composed of both public investment and consumption, as these are related to the planned growth. So reductions in the public expenditure can lead to reduced growth. However if these expenditures cannot be compensated by appropriate amount of public resources, budget deficit can create pressure on the price levels by increasing domestic excess, as supply cannot be increased in the short run in a planned economy due to lack of appropriate availabilities of imports. However, increased public borrowings need increased rate of interest which will increase the cost of borrowing for the private sector and reduce future growth and increase the price levels. If the increased level of public borrowings cannot generate public goods, future burden of repayments will increase. India is suffering from all these problems simultaneously as obvious from the historical data because the response of the authorities are of short run nature; as a result, the economy is going from 'boom to bust' without any definite direction towards improvements as far as financial policies are concerned. Government expenditures went up from Rs 205 bill in 1978 to Rs 396 bill in 1986. As a percentage of GDP it went up from .05 in 1978 to .08 in 1986. At the same time budget deficit as a percentage of GDP was increased from .06 in 1978 to .08 in 1986. However the control solutions do not provide much comfort. The budget deficit in the adaptive solution went up from Rs 72 bill in 1978 to Rs 167 bill in 1986. The reason is that the control solutions suggest we need to maintain the public borrowings at the same level but tax revenue as a percentage of the GDP should be reduced (it was .14 in 1978 and .16 in 1986 along the historical path, the corresponding figures along the adaptive control path should be .11 and .13 respectively). As a result the control solutions suggest higher levels of budget deficit. It may be due to the fact that lower tax rate can stimulate the economy (mainly the private sector) and it will create less pressure on prices (on the main form tax is the indirect tax) whereas the budget deficit working through the demand pressures will take some time to create its adverse effect in price levels. On the whole the control solution emphasis is on the public borrowings which were increasing at a very high rate during the latter periods, (i.e. 1983 - 1986) mainly due to the increasing public expenditures which went up from Rs 177 bill in 1978 to Rs 404 bill in 1986, and also due to the subsidies to the states (i.e. net lending LR). Net lendings went up from Rs 24.5 bill in 1978 to Rs 117 bill in 1986. The explanation can be found on the growth of real national income and the real domestic absorptions. If we want to maintain considerably high rate of growth of net income along with more or less constant rate of taxation, increased public debt will be the inevitable result. Certain structural changes are required (i.e. reduction of certain types of subsidies, e.g. transport subsidies which are designed to equalize cost of certain raw materials across the country) along with significant reductions of the government consumptions, but these are outside the scope of this model. However, the lesson is that structural changes through adjustment needs considerable financial restructuring and without an increased public debts it can put serious obstacles towards future growth prospects.

## Table 5.5
## Target paths
## (in 1987 price - billion Rs)

|      | A       | Y       | (X-M+FPT) | G      |
|------|---------|---------|-----------|--------|
| 1988 | 2358.94 | 3108.63 | -40.00    | 905.3  |
| 1989 | 2476.73 | 3264.03 | -38.00    | 950.5  |
| 1990 | 2730.76 | 3427.23 | -35.00    | 1002.5 |
| 1991 | 2867.31 | 3598.59 | -30.00    | 1018.0 |
| 1992 | 3010.67 | 3778.52 | -25.00    | 992.5  |
| 1993 | 3161.21 | 3967.47 | -20.00    | 1030.5 |
| 1994 | 3319.26 | 4165.81 | -20.00    | 1070.5 |
| 1995 | 3485.23 | 4374.10 | -20.00    | 1106.0 |
| 1996 | 3659.49 | 4592.81 | -20.00    | 1146.0 |

|      | TY    | LR    | FB-FP | CRD  | NHS    | GBS   |
|------|-------|-------|-------|------|--------|-------|
| 1988 | 498.0 | 142.7 | 30.0  | .12  | 1388.0 | 270.0 |
| 1989 | 554.0 | 154.0 | 30.5  | .12  | 1555.0 | 270.0 |
| 1990 | 616.0 | 175.0 | 31.5  | .11  | 1726.0 | 280.0 |
| 1991 | 646.0 | 200.0 | 32.5  | .11  | 1916.0 | 290.0 |
| 1992 | 678.0 | 219.0 | 33.5  | .11  | 2127.0 | 300.0 |
| 1993 | 714.0 | 238.0 | 34.5  | .11  | 2361.0 | 320.0 |
| 1994 | 749.0 | 265.0 | 36.5  | .10  | 2620.9 | 350.0 |
| 1995 | 787.0 | 289.0 | 36.0  | .10  | 2909.2 | 370.0 |
| 1996 | 826.0 | 315.0 | 35.0  | .10  | 3229.0 | 400.0 |

|      | NDA    | RR   | CD  | IR (%) | CI (%) | P (1987=100) | EXR (Rs/US $) |
|------|--------|------|-----|--------|--------|--------------|---------------|
| 1988 | 1006.0 | .103 | .9  | 9.5    | 9.0    | 108          | 13.9          |
| 1989 | 1166.0 | .103 | .9  | 9.5    | 9.0    | 116          | 16.0          |
| 1990 | 1294.0 | .103 | .9  | 9.5    | 9.0    | 125          | 17.0          |
| 1991 | 1437.0 | .103 | .9  | 9.5    | 8.5    | 136          | 17.0          |
| 1992 | 1595.0 | .103 | .9  | 9.5    | 8.5    | 146          | 17.0          |
| 1993 | 1770.0 | .103 | .9  | 9.5    | 8.5    | 158          | 17.0          |
| 1994 | 1965.0 | .103 | .9  | 9.5    | 8.0    | 171          | 17.0          |
| 1995 | 2181.0 | .103 | .9  | 9.5    | 8.0    | 185          | 17.0          |
| 1996 | 2421.0 | .103 | .9  | 9.5    | 8.0    | 199          | 17.0          |

## Table 5.6
### Optimal paths - experiment 1: emphasis on A
### (in 1987 price - billion Rs)

|      | A       | Y       | (X-M+FPT) | G      |
|------|---------|---------|-----------|--------|
| 1988 | 2365.62 | 3030.54 | -42.29    | 617.0  |
| 1989 | 2506.68 | 3147.87 | -35.51    | 673.71 |
| 1990 | 2737.09 | 3126.23 | -35.65    | 705.70 |
| 1991 | 2989.78 | 3261.52 | -34.01    | 741.13 |
| 1992 | 3001.67 | 3321.54 | -31.19    | 750.08 |
| 1993 | 3121.51 | 3431.37 | -29.09    | 778.59 |
| 1994 | 3291.25 | 3540.92 | -27.62    | 789.29 |
| 1995 | 3468.40 | 3688.08 | -25.65    | 893.07 |
| 1996 | 3502.19 | 3924.81 | -24.03    | 880.79 |

|      | TY    | LR     | FB-FP | CCR | NMS     | GBS    |
|------|-------|--------|-------|-----|---------|--------|
| 1988 | 485.5 | 240.01 | 32.09 | .11 | 1341.38 | 237.83 |
| 1989 | 534.1 | 245.32 | 31.51 | .11 | 1589.27 | 245.89 |
| 1990 | 531.4 | 240.50 | 25.50 | .10 | 1786.93 | 286.16 |
| 1991 | 560.9 | 252.32 | 25.65 | .10 | 1980.09 | 296.36 |
| 1992 | 581.1 | 268.06 | 24.71 | .10 | 2287.83 | 299.86 |
| 1993 | 596.9 | 275.76 | 22.80 | .10 | 2435.82 | 318.34 |
| 1994 | 601.8 | 284.44 | 21.67 | .10 | 2784.95 | 328.69 |
| 1995 | 645.4 | 289.09 | 20.51 | .10 | 3007.2  | 339.28 |
| 1996 | 674.9 | 305.85 | 19.75 | .11 | 3484.86 | 358.32 |

|      | NDA     | RR   | CD  | IR (%) | CI (%) | P (1987=100) | BD     | EXR (Rs/US $) |
|------|---------|------|-----|--------|--------|--------------|--------|---------------|
| 1988 | 1006.10 | .101 | .83 | 4.9    | 8.1    | 110          | 101.59 | 14.5          |
| 1989 | 1191.48 | .101 | .86 | 4.2    | 7.7    | 119          | 107.53 | 15.7          |
| 1990 | 1379.54 | .98  | .86 | 4.2    | 7.2    | 129          | 103.14 | 16.5          |
| 1991 | 1485.87 | .98  | .88 | 4.5    | 7.2    | 142          | 110.54 | 16.5          |
| 1992 | 1579.26 | .97  | .91 | 5.7    | 7.5    | 155          | 112.47 | 17.5          |
| 1993 | 1845.61 | .95  | .92 | 5.7    | 6.5    | 165          | 116.31 | 18.2          |
| 1994 | 2095.16 | .96  | .92 | 5.7    | 6.5    | 179          | 121.57 | 18.5          |
| 1995 | 2286.71 | .98  | .91 | 4.5    | 6.2    | 193          | 126.97 | 18.9          |
| 1996 | 2642.83 | .98  | .91 | 4.5    | 5.8    | 207          | 133.67 | 19.1          |

## Table 5.7
### Optimal paths: experiment 2: emphasis on P
### (in 1987 price - billion Rs)

|      | A       | Y       | (X-M+FPT) | G      |
|------|---------|---------|-----------|--------|
| 1988 | 2294.06 | 2569.36 | -41.05    | 636.94 |
| 1989 | 2431.82 | 2721.52 | -33.52    | 668.58 |
| 1990 | 2653.89 | 2975.47 | -34.60    | 699.43 |
| 1991 | 2809.06 | 3149.37 | -31.59    | 740.81 |
| 1992 | 2912.97 | 3261.28 | -28.25    | 753.31 |
| 1993 | 3029.37 | 3391.65 | -26.52    | 787.42 |
| 1994 | 3195.27 | 3576.34 | -26.45    | 821.09 |
| 1995 | 3365.96 | 3767.64 | -23.61    | 835.31 |
| 1996 | 3394.94 | 3804.57 | -22.54    | 821.30 |

|      | TY     | LR     | FB-FP | NMS     | CCR | GBS    |
|------|--------|--------|-------|---------|-----|--------|
| 1988 | 423.80 | 155.82 | 30.67 | 1282.07 | .13 | 231.24 |
| 1989 | 451.70 | 169.32 | 27.73 | 1501.23 | .13 | 246.02 |
| 1990 | 496.80 | 192.31 | 21.07 | 1669.97 | .12 | 265.69 |
| 1991 | 532.10 | 216.64 | 22.35 | 1867.01 | .12 | 285.35 |
| 1992 | 554.40 | 231.44 | 20.15 | 2160.88 | .12 | 291.45 |
| 1993 | 583.20 | 245.59 | 18.72 | 2380.95 | .13 | 307.18 |
| 1994 | 622.20 | 271.72 | 17.01 | 2661.09 | .13 | 325.78 |
| 1995 | 640.40 | 291.61 | 15.93 | 2058.62 | .12 | 335.08 |
| 1996 | 646.70 | 326.18 | 15.95 | 3230.70 | .13 | 347.41 |

|      | NDA    | RR   | CD   | IR (%) | CI (%) | P (1987=100) | BD     | EXR  |
|------|--------|------|------|--------|--------|--------------|--------|------|
| 1988 | 966.5  | .103 | .767 | 6.5    | 9.4    | 98.45        | 107.05 | 14.5 |
| 1989 | 1126.8 | .103 | .779 | 6.9    | 8.7    | 106.1        | 112.45 | 15.2 |
| 1990 | 1257.8 | .104 | .825 | 6.0    | 8.5    | 117.1        | 108.18 | 16.5 |
| 1991 | 1419.2 | .104 | .865 | 5.7    | 8.5    | 128.7        | 117.65 | 16.2 |
| 1992 | 1672.5 | .103 | .897 | 5.8    | 7.7    | 142.9        | 118.75 | 16.9 |
| 1993 | 1790.1 | .103 | .883 | 5.8    | 7.3    | 149.5        | 123.91 | 16.7 |
| 1994 | 2015.7 | .102 | .749 | 5.2    | 6.8    | 162.0        | 127.82 | 16.2 |
| 1995 | 2213.5 | .102 | .779 | 5.3    | 6.6    | 174.0        | 135.51 | 16.1 |
| 1996 | 2431.5 | .103 | .766 | 5.3    | 6.5    | 185.0        | 137.92 | 16.3 |

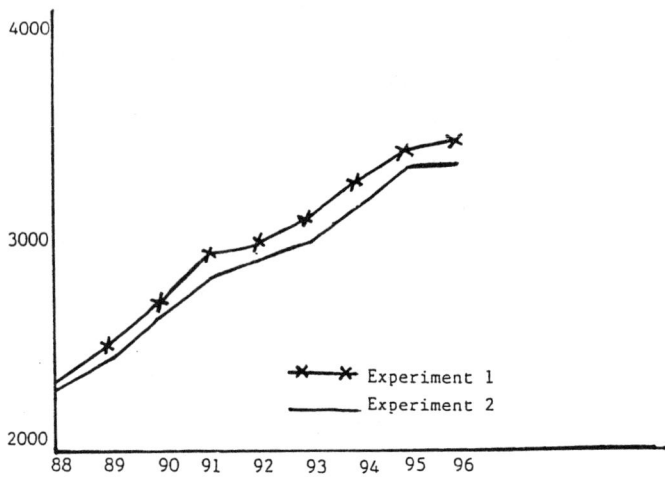

**Figure 5.1  Domestic Absorption (Rs billion)**

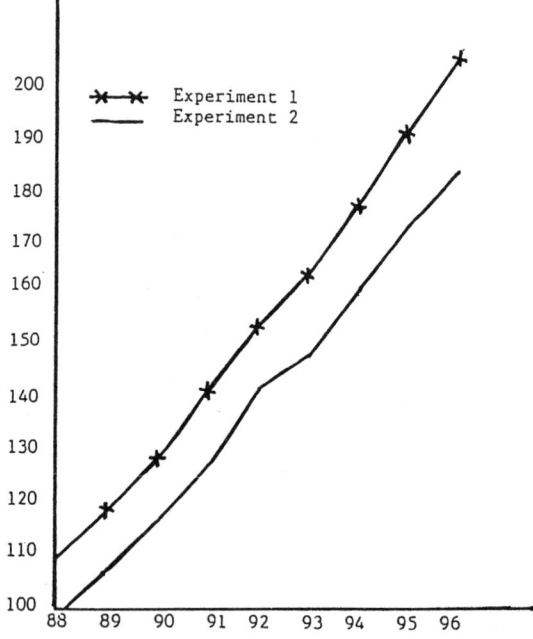

**Figure 5.2  Price Level**

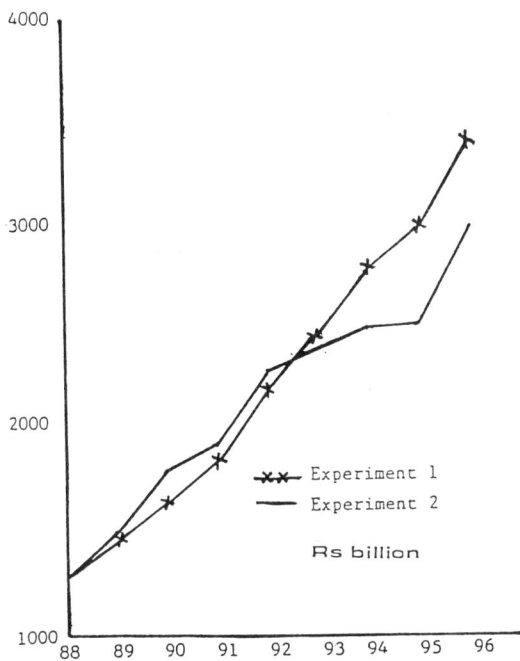

**Figure 5.3  Newly Created Money Stock**

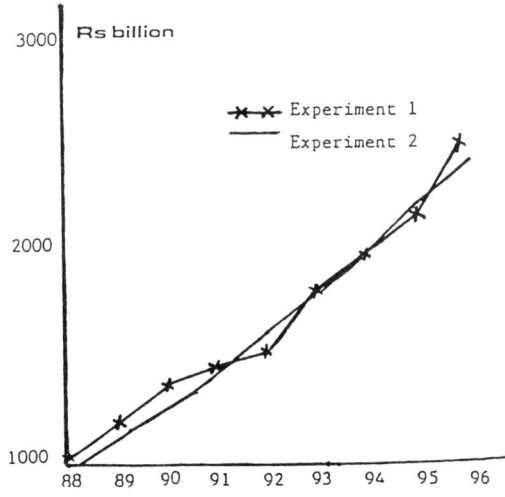

**Figure 5.4  Net Domestic Asset Creation**

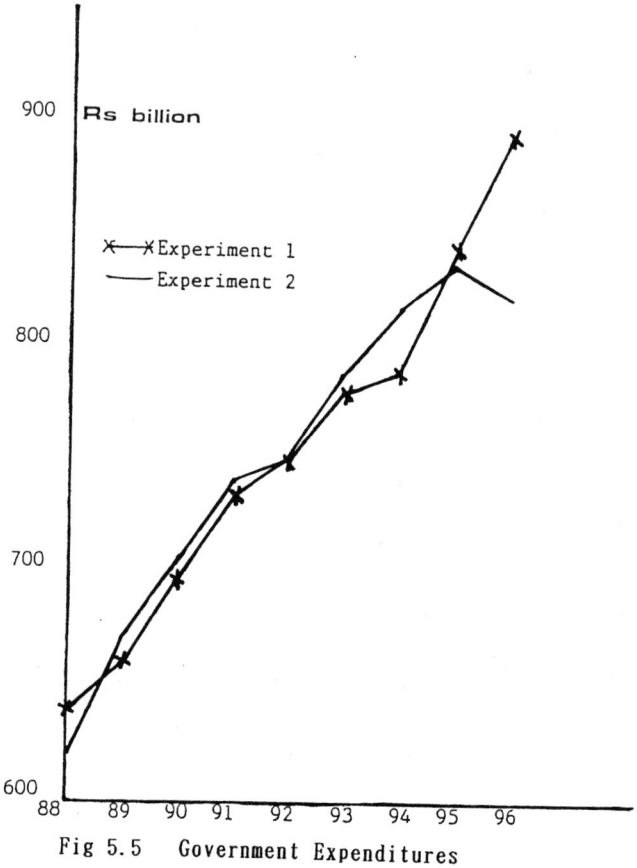

**Figure 5.5 Government Expenditure**

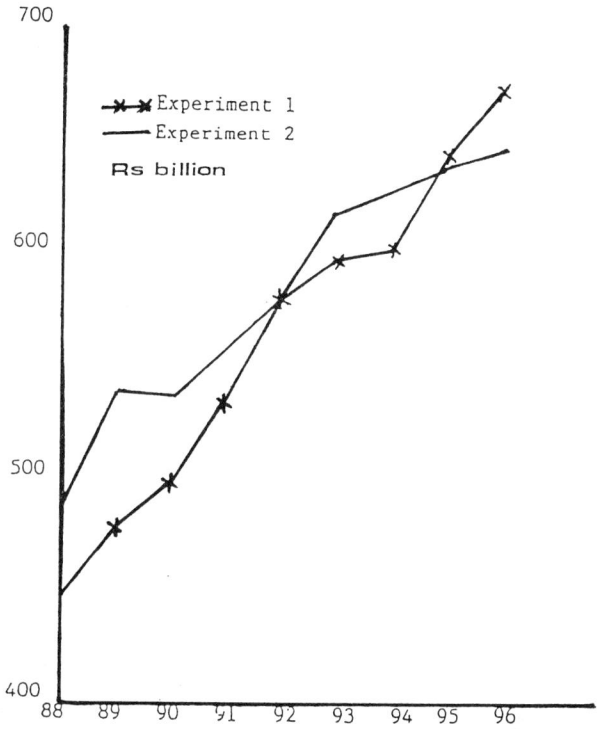

**Figure 5.6 Tax Revenues**

## Future planning 1988-1996

The essential purpose of any optimal control model is to plan for the future. The major difficulties the planner will face are, among others, the choices of the future paths of the exogenous variables and the target paths for the endogenous variable and their corresponding weights in the objective functions. In the adaptive control method weights are variables along with the parameters, so these are part of the solution process of the adaptive control. Once we select the weights for the initial period, the weights for the latter period can be determined along with the solutions. However, if we put more weights on any particular target, it will be reflected in the subsequent periods of planning as well. In the following experiments, two types of solutions are examined: (a) experiment 1: solution with emphasis on growth i.e. on domestic absorption; (b) experiment 2: solution with emphasis on price stability. Comparative performance of these two experiments are given below:

The targets paths are in table 5.5 and the optimal solutions are presented in tables 5.6 and 5.7. Target paths are selected accordingly to the judgement regarding the potentials of the Indian economy and the constraints it faces. Whereas target path each indicates, the national income and absorption are to grow at a rate of 5 per cent each in recent years (particularly between 1985-1990). Real national income grew at a rate of 6.5 per cent, but at a great cost of foreign borrowing and public indebtness. According to the target path net foreign borrowing will be more or less stable thus its share in the national income will be reduced. However, public expenditure and public domestic borrowings will increase from Rs 905 bill and Rs 270 bill in 1988 respectively to Rs 1146 bill and Rs 400 bill in 1986. Tax revenue will be increased from Rs 498 bill in 1988 to Rs 826 bill in 1996. Budget deficit will be more or less stable, thus its share in the real income will be reduced. Newly created money stock will grow at a rate of 11 per cent and major banking instruments like CD, RR, CI, and consequently IR will be stable over time. However, it is important to point out that the result will show some degree of underestimation regarding growth of real income and absorption because it is not possible for us to quantify the exact optimism and vigour of the private sector in a liberated economy.

*a) National income and domestic adsorption*

National income (GDP in constant 1987 price) and the domestic absorption will more or less be in the same way as indicated by the target path. The target paths for both the national income and the domestic absorption have 5 per cent rate of growth. The optimal solution, according to the experiment 1 suggests the national income will reach Rs 3126 bill in 1990, Rs 3431 bill in 1993 and Rs 3924 bill in 1996, whereas the target path suggests Rs 3427 bill in 1990, Rs 3967 bill in 1993 and Rs 4592 bill in 1996. The optional solution according to the experiment 2 suggests Rs 2975 bill in 1990, Rs 3391.65 in 1993 and Rs 3804 bill in 1996. The departure from the target paths can be explained by a number of variables influencing national income levels. Along the optimal path, government bond sales, tax revenues and budget deficits are less than those along the target path. At the same time trade deficits should be more along the optimal paths than along the target path. As a result domestic absorption follows the national income path, however the gap between the target domestic absorption and the optimal absorption are not very large mainly due to the fact that the gap between target trade balances and the optimal trade balances are not very large. These demonstrate that trade balance will play a very crucial role in domestic absorption compared to other domestic variables. Although interest rates along the optimal paths are less than those along the target paths, these have failed to stimulate domestic absorption effectively so as to counteract the negative effects of lower public borrowing and tax revenues. This perhaps demonstrates one of the most important characteristics of the Indian economy which is that the economy is more dependent on the public activities than private enterprises even when the obstructions for the private sectors are relaxed.

*b) Prices*

Prices along the optimal paths are less than those along the target path, although the differences are not always very significant. The optimal prices, according to the experiment 1 are 129 in 1990, 165 in 1993 and 207 in 1996 (with the base price for 1987 = 100); whereas according to the experiment 2, these are 117 in 1990, 149 in 1993 and 185 in 1996. If we look at the financial policy structures optimal government expenditures, government borrowing and tax revenues are not significantly different in these two experiments, however in experiment 2, interest rates, credit to deposit ratio, money supplies, central banks discount rate and reserve ratios of the commercial banks are at a much higher level than those along the experiment 1. At the same time, rate of devaluation along the experiment 1 is more than along the experiment 2, probably as a result trade deficits are less in the experiment 2 than in experiment 1. We may possibly draw the conclusion that monetary policies along with exchange rate can affect prices quite significantly, but given a more or less same financial policy structure, a harder monetary policy can affect growth prospects negatively although it will generate a more stable price level. Devaluation will induce price increases and price level will go up along with increased tax revenues.

*c) Balance of payments*

Net trade balance (X-IM+FPT) in the experiment 1 will go down from Rs 35 bill in 1990 to Rs 29 bill in 1995 and to Rs 24 bill in 1996. The corresponding figures in the experiments 2 are Rs 34 bill, Rs 26 bill and Rs 22 bill respectively. The reduction in the net trade deficit in experiment 2 can be attributed to the lower rate of devaluation compared to the experiment 1. Due to the fact that India's imports are mainly essential imports, there is little scope for their reduction through devaluation; on the other hand devaluation will increase import costs. India's exports may expand through devaluation, however in recent years there was no significant evidence in that respect. Exports are assumed to be exogenous so the positive influences of devaluation on exports cannot be reflected in this model.

The exchange rate should be considered as an expenditure switching policy because it works through alternative incentives for domestic supply of exports and imports substitutes and also on domestic expenditure on imports and exportable goods. Incentives are determined by the relative prices of traded goods in terms of domestic currency relative to the domestic costs of production and to the prices of nontraded goods. The floating exchange rate can make the currency too volatile. Part of the contributions of the exchange rate changes can be attributable to the plan-revisions and expenditure-switching process and can be carried out directly by shifting resources from importables to exportables. Managed exchange rate has a number of advantages in terms of stable investment regimes, absence of capital flight, and a stable demand – management policy in the domestic economy.

A number of authors have contributed to the theme that devaluations can leave a contractionary effect on domestic output (see Dias-Alejandro (1965); Krugman and Taylor (1978) and Hanson (1983)). When imports are essential for productions, devaluation can reduce the countries' ability to import and at the same time, a continuous fall in the value of the domestic currency contributes to inflationary expectations. In 1993, India has decided to float the currency and at the same time it has become fully convertible. The effects are yet to reflect on the real economy.

The reduction in the level of the net trade deficit will mean as a proportion to the real GDP, trade deficit will decline over time which will be reflected also in the declining ratio of net foreign borrowing to real GDP. However, that will not be any comfort due to the fact the accumulated trade deficit will create a substantial foreign debt at the end of the planning period.

*d) Monetary Policies*

Monetary and fiscal policies are interlinked in India. The monetary base will expand as the gap between public sector purchases of domestically produced goods and services and net revenues of the government is financed either by foreign debt or borrowings from the Reserve Bank of India. At the same time, the Reserve Bank can expand or contract the monetary base by altering the growth of credit to the banking system and the reserve requirements of the commercial banks or by changing the rate at which foreign exchange is available to the banking system. Monetary policy can affect the actual and desired composition of the private sector's portfolio. However, if the interest rate charged by the commercial banks is fixed by the Reserve Bank, the dynamics of portfolio choice of the private sector which can affect the interest rate is arrested. The increased availability of loans causes an increase in the implicit value of real assets relative to their production costs. Thus aggregate demand will be increased as a result of the increased demand for real assets. Similarly a reduction in the availability of credit will reduce aggregate demand.

If exchange controls are absent, as in the case from 1993 onwards in India, monetary policy can work in a different way. The private sector can now add foreign exchange to its portfolio of financial assets wither by retaining export receipts or by buying foreign exchange from the Reserve Bank. The Reserve Bank can no longer control the change in international reserve $\Delta R$, thus the power of the monetary policy to affect aggregate demand is reduced.

Regardless of exchange control system if sources of credit other than the banking system are limited, credit central by the Reserve Bank can be effective in influencing domestic spending and demand. That is the time when the linkages between the domestic and international financial markets are relatively weak. However, if links between the domestic and international financial markets are strong, control on the money supply can be an effective part of monetary policy when domestic prices are not linked to the world prices and there are a variety of non banking financial institutions providing credit which are subject to the ceiling imposed by the Reserve Bank. However, the Reserve Bank can control the reserve money supply if it can sterilize inflows of foreign exchanges unless the exchange rate is allowed to float freely. Some degree of intervention on the exchange rate is justified in order to combat the inflationary effect due to increased import costs in terms of domestic currency. Then the ability of the Reserve Bank to control monetary aggregates will be limited, rather it should try to control credit supplies in the banking system.

Monetary policy structure includes central banking policies, commercial banking policies and exchange rate policies. As can be seen in the balance of payments analysis, exchange rate can play a significant role in determining prices and the real output. In India imports are basically essential imports, so even announcements on devaluation can spread significant inflationary expectations. However, at the same time devaluation may make some of India's exports more attractive abroad. Considering these, a higher rate of devaluation can increase price level, but it may also improve the growth prospects. In experiment 1 we can see the effects of comparatively higher rate of devaluation (than in experiment 2). The results are higher national income, higher prices, higher balance of payment deficit and a higher level of foreign debt compared to that in experiment 2.

Regarding central banking policies, discount rate is slightly higher in the experiment 2 compared to that in experiment 1. The experiment 1 suggested that the discount rate should be 8.1 in 1988, 7.5 in 1992 and 5.8 in 1996. This suggests a both lower rate of discount and lower rate of market interest rate. In reality, the discount rate (CI) is almost constant and the market interest rate is almost as high as 20 per cent, these are all highly damaging for the further expansion of the private sector. Optimal solution in both of these experiments suggests a gradual decline of the CI and as a result market interest rate should be lower as well. In the experiment 1 the net domestic asset creation by the central bank (NDA) should go up from Rs 1006 bill in 1988 to Rs 1579 bill in 1992 and to Rs 2642 bill in 1996. The money supply should go up from Rs 1341 bill in 1988 to Rs 2287 bill in 1992 and to Rs 3484 in 1986 to experiment 1. In experiment 2, CI should be slightly higher and money supply should be slightly lower than in experiment 1, because of the emphasis on price stability in the experiment 2. As a result, the relationship between CI, NDA, the corresponding money supply and the price level are well established. Because of the emergence of the growing private sector, the relationship will be stronger in future as physical planning and fiscal policies will be less effective in future.

Regarding commercial bankings sector reserve ratio should be reduced and credit to deposit ratio should be increased (according to experiment 1), thus creating a situation of easier availability of credit which is a necessary precondition for the development of the private sector. However in experiment 2, we cannot see any reduction in the reserve ratio or any increase in the credit to deposit ratio except for a few years between 1990 to 1993, as a result money supply in experiment 2 will increase at a slower rate.

*Financial policies*

Public sector spending on currently produced goods and services is itself a component of total domestic spending and this adds to the domestic absorption. If public sector purchases are for domestically produced goods which are non-traded, it adds to the aggregate demand for domestic goods. At the same time, public investments on public enterprises add to the domestic total investments. A major part of the public expenditure in India is due to public enterprises. However, public sector imports and purchases of domestic goods which are exportables contribute to the import costs and can have negative impact on the longer run balance of payments if domestic production cannot go up as a result of these imports.

Public expenditure will go up from Rs 617 billion in 1988 to Rs 750 billion in 1992 and to Rs 880 billion in 1996. The corresponding figures for the lending to the States will go up from Rs 240 billion in 1988 to Rs 268 billion in 1992 and to Rs 305 billion in 1996. The financing of this expenditure can affect an economy in a variety of ways: to the extent that the increased public spending will increase equal tax liability for the private sector either in the present through tax financing or in future owing to finance public debt, current or future private disposable income would be reduced. However, if the discount rates applied to further tax liabilities are sufficiently large, the effect on current spending can be small.

Tax revenues should go up from Rs 485 billion in 1988 to Rs 581 billion in 1992 and to Rs 674 billion in 1996. The other form of financing is the Government bond sales which will go up from Rs 237 billion in 1988 to Rs 299 billion in 1992 and to Rs 358 billion in 1996. The relationships between the public expenditure policies and the monetixation of the deficits are very close; the net domestic asset creation by the central bank will increase from Rs 1006 billion in 1988 to Rs 2642 billion in 1996 as a result of the budget deficit which is increasing throughout.

The deficit of the public sector can be used as a stimulus to aggregate demand. The endogeneity of tax receipts implies that fiscal outcome may be controlled imperfectly. Public sector spending on imports, payments on interest abroad and net transfers from abroad may have substantial impact on fiscal deficits.

If we compare the outcome of the alternative experiments, the slight reduction in price inflation in the second experiment can be achieved by a reduction in public expenditure and growth rates, but the budget deficit will not be affected much. Thus the correspondence between the size of the public sector deficit and the changes in the magnitude of the public sector's stimulus to aggregate demand may be inexact.

## Foreign borrowing

A sustainable balance of payment deficits and foreign debts needs decisions regarding the country's ability to obtain and use in productive purposes any resources available from abroad. For that purpose the value of net exports of goods and services must match sufficiently to service foreign debts without reducing the essential imports required to support domestic growth. A country can borrow from abroad if the rate of return from the wages over the time period during which resources are available can sufficiently finance the cost of borrowings. It is also optimal to use foreign debt to mark consumptions overtime in the fall of various internal and external shocks (see Williamson, 1973). Normally we assume that the ratios like debt to export or debt to gross national product can indicate the country's sustainabilities. However, there are problems. The country can employ debt successfully for production purposes and if the ratio of foreign savings is much higher than the domestic savings, then the debt to export ratio will be high compared to a country when the capacity to utilize foreign savings is restricted due to the country's structural inability to absorb productive resources. As a result, we cannot say what is the desirable level of these ratios, these will vary from country to country. What is undesirable is to have structural break, where these ratios can go explosively; that has been the situation in India since 1985.

Devaluation in these circumstances may create special problems. The devaluation increases the share of national income needed to finance interest payment on foreign debt, which can reduce domestic output (see van Wijnbergen, 1986). Devaluation can also cause fiscal imbalances. Due to devaluation, domestic currency equivalence of interest payments on foreign debts and import costs of the public sectors may have explosive growths, which may cause serious fiscal deficits (see Ize and Ortiz, 1987). As a result, the government may have to increase taxes, reduce subsidies and increase its borrowings from the Reserve Bank, i.e. inflationary financing. Due to higher inflation, nominal interest rate may have to go up as well. What is needed is a desirable balance between the financial planning, devaluation and foreign debts.

Foreign borrowing according to the optimal path should go down from Rs 32.09 bill in 1988 to Rs 24.71 bill in 1992 and to Rs 19.75 in 1996. In India's case, foreign borrowing is a means of financing public expenditures, and is limited due to the accumulated debt. Table 5.8 shows the details regarding India's foreign debt situation.

Table 5.8
Foreign debt (according to experiment 1 - billion Rs)

|      | debt/GDP | debt exports service | interest/exports payments | foreign exchange import coverage (months) |
|------|----------|----------------------|---------------------------|-------------------------------------------|
| 1988 | 07.0     | 40.1                 | 9.4                       | 2.8                                       |
| 1989 | 17.4     | 39.0                 | 8.7                       | 2.8                                       |
| 1990 | 18.1     | 37.3                 | 8.8                       | 2.8                                       |
| 1991 | 18.7     | 38.3                 | 9.3                       | 2.7                                       |
| 1992 | 19.0     | 38.3                 | 9.6                       | 2.7                                       |
| 1993 | 18.7     | 39.5                 | 9.6                       | 2.5                                       |
| 1994 | 18.5     | 39.8                 | 9.5                       | 2.8                                       |
| 1995 | 18.3     | 38.1                 | 9.4                       | 3.0                                       |
| 1996 | 18.1     | 37.5                 | 9.4                       | 3.2                                       |

Table 5.9 - Underlying assumptions on debt service

|      | three month Eurodollar annual interest rate (%) | average interest rate on debt paid by India** | foreign investment (US $) ** million |
|------|-------------------------------------------------|-----------------------------------------------|--------------------------------------|
| 1988 | 6.4                                             | 4.0                                           | 382                                  |
| 1989 | 7.2                                             | 3.7                                           | 525                                  |
| 1990 | 7.5                                             | 3.8                                           | 613                                  |
| 1991 | 7.8                                             | 4.0                                           | 760                                  |
| 1992 | 7.9                                             | 4.2                                           | 908                                  |
| 1993 | 8.2                                             | 4.5                                           | 1050                                 |
| 1994 | 8.2                                             | 4.8                                           | 1130                                 |
| 1995 | 8.1                                             | 4.8                                           | 1220                                 |
| 1996 | 8.0                                             | 4.8                                           | 1270                                 |

\* Average interest rate paid includes prices.
\*\* At the optimum rate according to experiment 1.

We assume India has to pay a higher interest rate in future, due to worldwide credit shortages, however, due to a liberated atmosphere there will be more foreign investment which until 1986-87 was almost nil. The result shows that the debt to GDP will be almost constant over the period, thus creating continuous pressures on the economy. The debt service to export will not be reduced either, that demonstrates the weakness of India's export efforts which will take a long period to overcome. The ratio of interest payment to export will not go down either, as a result ability to import will still be limited over the planning period, that will be the reason for slow growth despite the liberated atmosphere.

## Concluding comments

The development process of an economy is a complex one. Liberalization can help in certain aspects, but at the same time lack of finance can inhibit growth. The optimal solution derived in this research shows clearly there is a need to have a less repressive credit regime though successive reductions in the stringency of the commercial banking instruments to make credit available easily to the industrial sector without a prohibitive interest rate system. At the same time public expenditure can be financed through taxations, reductions in lending for non planned expenditures and through public borrowing. However, public borrowing should have a limit, otherwise total public debt will go beyond any acceptable limit and as a result tax rates should have to go up. Foreign borrowing as a source of finance has a limited capacity for India, that is also true about foreign investment. So India has to depend on its own resources, which will restrict the growth rate due to the increasing need to import and the lower rate of growth of exports.

The advantages of an adaptive control system is quite obvious. The control system can tell us where the constraints are and what is possible on a realistic basis rather than drawing up a plan which does not take into account the people's reaction to the policies. The important characteristics of development planning in the changed situation are that the private sector will take increasingly important role in the total economic activity and the physical controls of the planning commission will be substantiated or substituted by the banking and financial controls. In an adaptive control system, we are in a position to quantify reactions of the private sectors in that changed atmosphere, by examining the reaction parameters of the control system on their dynamics in relation to the changing expectation and achievements of planning.

# Bibliography

Alesina, Alberto, 'Alternative Monetary Regimes', *Journal of Monetary Economics*, **21**, 1988, pp. 175–183.

Aoki, H.J., *Optimisation of Stochastic Systems* Academic Press, New York, 1967.

Astrom, K.J., *Introduction to Stochastic Control Theory*, Academic Press, New York, 1970.

Bacha, E.L., 'A Three Gap Model of Foreign Transformers and the G.D.P. growth rate in Developing Countries', *Journal of Dev. Econ.*, **32**, 1990, pp. 279–296.

Balassa, B., 'Adjustment Policies in Developing Countries. A Reassessment' *World Development*, vol. **12** no. 9, September 1984.

Balassa, B., and McCarthy, F.D., 'Adjustment Policies in Developing Countries', 1979–83; an update; World Bank. **675** 1984

Barro, Robert, J., 'Are Government Bonds Net Wealth?', *Journal of Political Economy*, vol. **82**, Nov-Dec 1974, pp. 1095–1117.

Barro, Robert J., and Gordon, David B., 'Rules, Discretion and Reputation in a model of monetary policy', *Journal of Monetary Economics*, vol. **12**, 1983, pp. 101–21.

Bar-Shalom and Sivan, R., 'On the Optimal Control of Discrete-Time Linear Systems with Random Parameters', IEEE Trans. on Automatic Control, AC-14, No.1, February 1969.

Basu, Dipak, 'Sequential control of a Monetary Policy Model for India', *International Journal of System Science*, July, 1986.

Basu, Dipak, 'IMF Programme and the Developing World: Case Studies on Egypt and Nigeria', *Middle East & African Review*; June 1987.

Basu, D., and Balasubramanium, V., 'India: Export Subsidies and Export Performances' in C. Milner (ed), *Export Strategies and Export Performance*, Harvester-Wheatshaft, New York, 1991.

Basu, D., and Lazaridis, A., 'Evaluation of International Investment Allocation in India', *International Journal of System Sciences*, vol. **11**, no. 7, pp. 889–906, 1980.

Basu, D., and Lazaridis, A., 'Stochastic Optimal Control by Psendo-Inverse', *Review of Economics and Statistics*, vol. **LXV**, no. 2 , pp. 346–351, 1983.

Basu, D., and Lazaridis, A., 'Method of Stochastic Optimal Control by Bayesian Filtering Techniques', *International Journal of System Sciences*, vol. **17**, no. 1 , pp. 81–5, 1986.

Bhagwati, Jagdish, N. and Padma Desai, India: *Planning for Industrialisation*, Oxford University Press, New Delhi, 1970.

Box, G.E.P., and Pearce, D.A., 'Distribution of residual autocorrelations in autoregressive-integrated moving average time series models', *Journals of the American Statistical Association*, **65**, 1970, pp. 1509–26.

Bhagawti, Jagdish, N. and Srinivasan, T.N., *Foreign Trade Regimes and Economic Development:* India, NBER, New York and Columbia Univ. Press, 1975.

Brahmananda, P.R., 'Economic theory, Indian planning experience and beyond', Indian Statistical Institute, Bangalore, November, 1981.

Branson, W., 'Economic structure and policy for external balance". *IMF Staff Papers*, March 1983.

Buchanan, James, M., *Public Principles of Public Debt: A Defence and Restatement* (Homewood, Illinois, R.D. Irwin, 1958)

Buiter, Willem, 'Monetary, Financial and Fiscal Policies Under Rational Expectations', *IMF Staff Papers*, **27**, 1980.

Buiter, W., and Patel, U., 'Debt, deficits and Inflation: an application to the Public finances of India', *Jounral of Public Economics*, **47**, 1992, pp. 171–205.

Calro, Guillermo A., 'Costly Trade Liberalizations: Durable goods and capital mobility', *International Monetary Fund Staff Papers*, Washington, Vol. **35** September 1988, pp. 461–73.

Chow, G., *Analysis and Control of Dynamic Economic Systems*, Wiley, New York, 1975.

Chow, G., *Econometric Analysis by Control Methods*, Wiley, New York, 1981.

Cline, W.R., 'Exchange rate policies for less developed countries in the world of floating rates', *Essays in International Finance* no. 199, Princeton University, 1978.

Connors, M.M., 'Controllability of Discrete Linear Random Dynamical Systems', SIAM *Journal of Control*, May, 1967.

Craine, R., and Havenner, A., 'Estimation Analogies in Control and Econometrics', unpublished paper, University of California, Berkeley, 1977.

Das, M., and Cristi, R., 'Robustness of an Adaptive Pole Placement Algorithm in the Presence of Bounded Disturbances and Slow Time Variation of Parameters', *IEEE Transactions on Automatic Control*, vol. **35**, no 6, June 1990.

Diaz-Alejandro, Carlos, *Exchange Rate and Devaluation in a Semi-Industrialised Country: The Experience of Argentian, 1955-1961*, Cambridge, Mass., M.I.T. Press, 1965.

Franco, G.H.B., 'Fiscal Reforms and Stabilisation', *Economic Journal* vol. **100** no. 399, pp. 176-188, March 1990.

Goldberger, A.C., Nager, A.L. and Odeh, H.S., 'The covariance matrices of reduced-form coefficients and of forecasts for a structural econometric model', *Econometrica*, **29**, 1961.

Goldstein, M., 'The Global Effects of Funds supported adjustment programmes', IMF Occasional Paper no. 42, 1986.

Grenville, T.N.E., 'Some applications of the psendo-inverse of a matrix', *Saim Review*, **2**, pp. 15-22, 1960.

Hanson,. J.A., 'Contrationary Devaluation, Substitution in Production and consumption and the Role of the Labour Market', *Journal of International Economics*, vol. **14**, Feb, 1983, pp. 179-89.

Hazra, S., 'Capital and Technological Progress in the Indian Economy, 1950-51 - 1980-81', Birla Institute of Scientific Research, New Delhi, 1985.

Householder, A.S., *Principles of Numerical Analysis*, McGraw Hill, New York, 1953.

Hussain, N.H., and Thirwall, A.P., 'The IMF supply-side approach to devaluation: An assessment with reference to Sadan', *Oxford Bulletin and Econ and Stat*, **46**, 2, 1984.

Intrilligator, M.D., *Mathematical Optimisation and Economic Theory*, Prentice-Hall, 1971.

Ize, Alain, and Ortiz, G., 'Fiscal Rigidities, Public Debt and Capital Flight', *IMF Staff Papers*, vol. **34**, June 1987.

Joshi, V., and Little, I.M.D., 'Indian Macro Economic Policies', *Indian Economic Review*, vol. **xxii** no. 9, 1988.

Kalman, R.E., 'A new approach to linear filtering prediction problem', *Journal of Basic Engineering*, Trans, **82D**, 1960.

Kendrick, D., 'Caution and probing - in macroeconomic models', *Journal of Economic Dynamics and Control*, **4**, 1982.

Kendrick, D., *Stochastic Control for Economic Models*, McGraw Hill, New York, 1982.

Keynes, John Maynard, *A Tract on Monetary Reform*, London, 1923.

Khan Mohsin, S., 'A Monetary Model of Balance of Payments: The case of Venezuela', *Journal of Monetary Economics*, **2**, 1976, pp. 311-332.

Khan Mohsin S., and Knight, Malcolm D., 'Stabilisation programs in developing countries: A formal framework', *International Monetary Fund Staff Papers*, March, 1981, pp. 1-53.

Khan Mohsin S., and Lizondo, J. Saul, 'Devaluation, fiscal deficits and the real exchange rate', *World Bank Economic Review*, Jan, 1987, pp. 357-374.

Khan, Mohsin S., and Montiel, Peter J., 'Grown Oriented Adjustment Programs', *International Monetary Fund Staff papers*, vol. **36**, no. 2, June 1989, pp. 279–295.

Khan, Mohsin S., Montiel, Peter, and Haque, Nadeem U., 'Adjustment with Growth', *Journal of Development Economics*, **32**, 1990, pp. 155–179.

Killick, T., 'The Quest for Economic Stabilization', The IMF and the Third World: London. Heinemann, 1984.

Krugman, P., and Taylor, L., 'Contrationary Effects of Devaluation', *Journal of International Economics*, vol. **8**, August 1978, pp. 445–56.

Kusner, H.J., *Stochastic Stability and Control*, Academic Press, New York, 1967.

Leiderman, Lernardo, and Blegen, Mario I., 'Modelling and Testing Ricardian Equivalence', *International Monetary Fund Staff Papers*, 1989, pp. 1–35.

Lucas, R.E.B., 'Liberalization of Indian Trade and Industrial Licensing', *Journal of Development Economics* **31**, pp. 141–175, 1989.

Lucas, R.E.B., India's Industrial Policy in Lucas, R.E.B. and Gustav Papanek (ed). *The Indian Economy: Recent Development and Future Prospects*, West View Press, Boulder and London, 1988.

Lucas, Robert E. Jr., 'Money in a Theory of Finance', *Carnagie-Rochester Series on Public Policy*, (Amsterdam), vol. **21**, (Autumn), 1984, pp. 9–55.

Mahalanobis, P.C., 'Some observations on the process of growth of national income', Sankhya, September, 1953.

Mason, Paul R., 'The Sustainability of Fiscal Deficits', *Staff Papers, International Monetary Fund*, (Washington), vol. **32**, 1985, pp. 577–605.

Mathieson, Donald J., 'The Impact of Monetary and Fiscal Policy Under Flexible Exchange Rates and Alternative Expectation Structure', *International Monetary Fund Staff Papers*, 1978, pp. 535–570.

McCallum, Bennett T., 'Are Bond-Financed Deficits Inflationary? A Richardian Analysis', *Journal of Political Economy*, vol. **92**, (Feb), 1984, pp. 123–35.

Miller, Marcus, 'Inflation-Adjusting the Public Sector Financial Deficit', in, *1982 Budget*, ed. by John Kay (Oxford: Basil Blackwell) 1982.

Minhas, B.S., 'The Planning Process and Annual Budgets', *Indian Economic Review*, vol. **xxii** no. 2, pp. 115–149, 1988.

Nambiar, R., and Mechta, R., 'Price competitiveness of Indian Manufacturing Industry', *Economic & Policital Weekly*, pp. 1278–1284, June 18, 1988.

Nashashibi, K., 'A supply framework for exchange reform in developing countries. The experience of Sudan', *IMF Staff Papers*, March 1986.

Oliverra, J.H.G., 'Money, prices and fiscal lags - a note on the dynamics of inflation', *Banca Nazionale del Lavoro Quarterly Review* no. **82** pp. 258–67, Sept, 1967.

Penrose, R., 'A generalised Inverse for matrices', *Proceedings of the Cambridge Philosophical Society*, **51**, pp. 406–413, 1955.

Penrose, R., 'On the Best Approximate Solution of Linear Matrix Equations', *Proceedings of the Cambridge Philosophical Society*, **52**, pp. 17–19, 1956.

Pindyck, R.S., 'Optimal Planning for Economic Stabilization', North Holland, 1973.

Polak. Jacques, J., 'Monetary Analysis of Income Formation and Payments Problem', *International Monetary Fund Staff Papers*, Nov, 1957, pp. 1–50.

Pontrayagin, L.S., Boltyanskii, V.G., Gamkerlidze, R.V. and Mischenko, E.E., 'The Mathematical theory of Optimal Processes', tran by Trirogoff, K.N., New York, *Interscience Pub.*, 1962.

Rao, V.K.R.V., *India's National Income*, 1950–1980, New Delhi Sage Publication, 1983.

Ricardo, David, 'On The Principles of Political Economy and Taxation', vol. I of the work and correspondence of David Ricardo, ed. by Piers Sraffa (Cambridge University Press), 1951.

Rodriguez, Carlos A., 'A Stylized model of the Devaluation-Inflation Spiral', *International Monetary Fund Staff Papers*, vol. **25**, (March), 1978, pp. 76–89.

Sau, R., 'The Green Revolution and Industrial Growth in India', *Economic and Political Weekly* pp. 789–796 April 16, 1988.

Siermann, C.L.J., and Haan, J.D., 'On sustainability and political determinants of government debt in devleoping coutnries', *Rivista Internazionale di Scienze Economiche e Commerciali*, vol **XL**, no 1, 1993, pp. 81–92.

Sims, Christopher A., 'Policy Analysis with Econometric Models', *Brookings Papers on Economic Activity*, **I**, 1982, pp. 107–135.

Spaventa, Luigi, 'The Growth of Public Debt', *International Monetary Fund Staff Papers*, 1988, pp. 374–399.

Tanzi, V., 'Inflation and the measurement of fiscal deficits', *IMF Staff Papers* vol. **34** no. 4, pp. 711–38, December, 1987.

Tanzi, V., 'The Impact of Macroeconomic Policies on the level of Taxation and the Fiscal Balance in Developing Countries', *International Monetary Fund, Staff Papers*, vol. **36**, no. 3, (September) 1989, pp. 633–656.

Tsakalis, K., and Ioannou, P., 'A new indirect adaptvie control scheme for time varying plants', *IEEE Transactions on Automatic Control*, vol. **35**, no 6, June 1990.

Tse, Edison and Michael, Athans, 'Adaptive Stochastic Control for a class of linear system', *IEEE transaction on Automatic Control*, **AC-17**, pp. 38–52, 1972.

Waud, Roger, 'Proximate Targets and Monetary Policy', *Economic Journal*, March 1973, pp. 1–20.

van Wijnbergen, S., 'Exchange Rate Management and Stabilization Policies in Developing Countries', in *Economic Adjustment and Exchange Rates in*

*Developing Countries*, edited by Edwards, S., and Ahmed, L., University of Chicago Press, 1986.

Williamson, J., 'A survey of the literature on the offical Peg', *Journal of Development Economics* August 1982.

Williamson, J.H., 'Payment Objectives and Economic Welfare', *IMF Staff Papers*, vol. **20**, November 1973, pp. 573–90.

# INDEX

| | |
|---|---|
| Adaptive Control | 69, 87, 142 |
| Asset Creation | 89, 101, 109-110, 118-120, 127-129 |
| Banking Policies | 16, 25-29, 31-33, 101 |
| Balance of Payments | 15, 38, 91, 96, 103, 109, 123, 124, 136 |
| Budget Constraints | 56, 92-96, 100, 139 |
| Budget Deficit | 56, 91, 109, 125 |
| | |
| Central Discount Rate | 89, 101, 109-110, 116, 138 |
| Certainty Equivalence | 68 |
| Chile | 21, 55 |
| China | 39, 42 |
| Central Bank | 101, 109, 123, 137 |
| Characteristic-roots | 111 |
| Commercial Bank | 101, 109, 137, 138 |
| Controllability | 78, 79 |
| | |
| Debt Service | 15, 38, 141 |
| Devaluation | 15, 39, 43, 54, 112, 116 |
| Deterministic Control | 57 |
| Domestic Absorption | 34, 57, 100, 109, 116, 122 |
| Domestic Demand | 15, 21, 100, 109 |
| | |
| Exchange Rate | 36, 43, 50-52, 82, 83m 109, 136 |
| Exchange Control | 109, 116, 124, 137 |
| Exports | 15, 39, 41, 44, 48, 96, 97, 103, 125, 136 |
| | |
| Fiscal Dynamics | 91, 116 |
| Fiscal Policy | 33, 85, 92, 93, 109, 138 |
| First Plan | 23 |
| Fifth Plan | 30 |
| Filter | 73, 77 |
| Financial Policies | 27, 29, 30, 34, 138 |
| Fourth Plan | 28 |
| Foreign Borrowings | 109, 139 |
| Foreign Debt | 36, 38, 140, 141 |
| Foreign Trade | 44, 109, 136 |
| Foreign Investment | 141 |
| | |
| Government Expenditure | 91, 100, 109, 112, 116, 139 |
| GDP | 15, 21, 100, 109, 122 |

| | |
|---|---|
| Industry | 19, 37, 39, 44, 48, 49 |
| Interest Rate - Domestic | 84, 93, 102, 116, 124, 135 |
| Interest Rate - European | 141 |
| Imports | 15, 38, 96, 97, 103, 125, 136 |
| Investments | 49 |
| IMF | 49, 51, 54, 55, 98 |
| | |
| Korea | 39, 42 |
| | |
| Licencing Systems | 18 |
| | |
| Malaysia | 39, 42 |
| Monetary Policy | 34, 84, 89, 101, 116, 118, 199, 120, 121, 123, 127-129, 131, 137 |
| Money Supply | 22-28, 34, 82, 86-89, 92-94, 101-110, 116, 123, 137 |
| Money Stock | 24-28, 34, 82, 89, 92, 94, 101-102, 109 |
| Monetary Dynamics | 91, 116 |
| | |
| Optimal Control | 58, 59, 62, 67, 70, 71 |
| | |
| Price Level | 22, 25-28, 34, 86, 97, 100-102, 109, 110, 116, 123, 135 |
| Public Expenditure | 109, 139 |
| Public Sector | 49, 96, 99, 138 |
| Pseudo-Inverse | 65, 69, 78 |
| | |
| Rules vs Discretion | 68 |
| Response Multipliers | 111, 112 |
| | |
| Seventh Plan | 34 |
| Sixth Plan | 31 |
| Structural Adjustments | 55, 56 |
| Stochastic Control | 65, 69, 78 |
| Stochastic Simulation | 62 |
| | |
| Tax Revenue | 36, 95, 100, 109, 139 |
| Tax Rate | 36, 95, 100, 109, 126 |
| Third Plan | 26 |